BUDDHISM IN TRANSITION

BUDDHISM IN TRANSITION

by DONALD K. SWEARER

The Westminster Press
Philadelphia

PUBLISHED BY THE WESTMINSTER PRESS
PHILADELPHIA, PENNSYLVANIA ®

PRINTED IN THE UNITED STATES OF AMERICA

TO NANCY

CONTENTS

ACKNOWLEDGMENTS

The author wishes to thank the Danforth Foundation, the Society for Religion in Higher Education, and Oberlin College for the financial assistance that enabled us to spend the year 1967–1968 studying in Asia. I also wish to acknowledge support and help from Professors Philip Ashby and Kenneth Ch'en of Princeton University; Professors K. N. Jayatilleke, W. S. Karunaratna, and J. Dhirasekera of the University of Ceylon; Nyanaponika Thera and Richard Abeyasekera of the Buddhist Publication Society, Kandy, Ceylon; Khun Sulak Sivarakasa, Bhikkhu Khantipālo, Bhikkhu Buddhadāsa, Phra Mahā Prayuddha, and Phra Mahā Sīla of Thailand; Professor Yoneo Ishii, Kyoto University; Professor M. Doi, Doshisha University; Professor M. Abe, Nara Women's College; and S. Kobori, Ryokoin Temple, Kyoto, Japan; and many other friends who were so kind and helpful to us during our months in Ceylon, Thailand, and Japan. Much of the material contained in these chapters was delivered as a lecture series at the Chautauqua Institute in the summer of 1969 at the kind invitation of Dr. Herbert Gezork, President Emeritus of Andover Newton Theological School and currently Chairman of the Department of Religion at Chautauqua.

INTRODUCTION

Rapid technological and scientific change and the consequent problems it raises in the social, political, and economic spheres encompass all of us. Institutions as well as
individuals must deal with questions of progress and
change, development and modernization. Change may be
rejected, accommodated, or affirmed, but it cannot be ignored. Organized religion, whether in the West or in the
East, is no exception to this rule. The challenges and tensions currently so typical of religion in the United States
and Europe are evidenced in the religions of Asia as well,
in particular Southeast Asian Buddhism. It is the purpose
of these chapters to examine Buddhism in transition especially within its Southeast Asian cultural context. East Asia
raises special problems. Buddhism in China has been
largely eclipsed by Maoist Communism, although many
aspects of the Buddhist revival in Southeast Asia in the
first quarter of this century were paralleled in China.[1] Occasional references will be made to Japan, but neither the
efforts of traditional Buddhist groups to adjust to the contemporary world nor the fascinating development of the
numerous new religions in Japan will be discussed at

length. Our focus on Southeast Asia (including Ceylon) is appropriate, we think, both because in much of this region Buddhism holds the key to future stability and progress and, also, because the Buddhism of different Southeast Asian countries shares the same Theravāda form (with the notable exception of Vietnam). Before examining some of the fundamentals of this form of Buddhism, some preliminary comments must be made about the problem of religion and change.

The problem of religion and change is immensely complex. Sociologists such as Talcott Parsons and Robert Bellah investigate it from the perspective of the social sciences, while others like Harvey Cox or Colin Williams take their stance primarily as theologians and churchmen. Although approaches vary, there is a certain degree of unanimity in some of the questions asked: What is the most appropriate balance between continuity and change? How can religion as a cultural gyroscope maintain its balance in the face of change? In what sense can religion continue to represent the limit images of personal and social identity and at the same time participate in the very reality it is defining? The problem of religion and change, though intensified in times of rapid development, is incipient in every age. The crux of the problem rests in the nature of the dialectic between religion and its cultural society.

We do not mean to imply that religion exists separately from its cultural society; however, religion as a pattern of normative symbols representing the nature of reality depends for its integrity on more than patterns of culture. It is precisely because religious symbols "suggest what reality ultimately is, what the source of order (and often of disorder) in the universe is, what sort of authority in the most general terms is acceptable to men, and what sorts of action by individuals make sense in such a world" [2] that re-

ligion is so decisively important in transitional periods such
as the present. It is from such a perspective that we speak
of the dialectical relationship between religion and its cultural society. The strength or weakness of this dialectic is
partly a matter of perspective. In Christian cultures, for
example, the ideal religious life is described as living *in* the
world but not being *of* the world; nevertheless, from a sociological perspective no one would dispute the fact that
Christianity is a major social institution inextricably involved in mundane affairs.[3]

Theologians as well as sociologists have addressed themselves to the question of the tension between religion and
its cultural society. H. Richard Niebuhr, although influenced by social philosophy and sociology, was speaking as
a Christian theologian when he described the dialectic
between Christ and culture in terms of five motifs: Christ
against culture, the Christ of culture, Christ above culture,
Christ and culture in paradox, and Christ the transformer
of culture.[4] At one extreme is the view that holds the authority of religious claims to be absolute and resolutely
rejects culture's claims to loyalty. At the other extreme is
the position in which religion and its sociocultural milieu
are so homogenized as to be nearly indistinguishable. In
the latter, culture is interpreted through Christ and Christ
is understood through culture with no great tension between church and world.[5] In between these two extreme
approaches Niebuhr places three intermediate positions.
Each of them builds from the dialectic between the religious and the cultural rather than abrogating or avoiding
it. All three take the religious reality (i.e., Christ, God in
Christ) to be somehow "other" than culture but disagree
about the manner in which the two are related. The three
views include the synthesis of the religious and the cultural in a churchman like Thomas Aquinas, the paradoxi-

cal dualism between the two in the thought of a Paul or a
Luther, and the conversion or transformation of culture by
Christ in the Logos doctrine of the Gospel of John or Au-
gustine's vision of the City of God.

The starting point is the tension between the religious
and its sociocultural milieu. Some would suggest that new
religious realities bring about cultural change. Others
would defend the view that changes in religious realities
are largely determined by changes in the sociocultural context. Whereas, in any given situation, the primary causal
force might be a matter of argument, the rapidity of modern technological advancement is not a problem for dispu-
tation. In the light of this fact, the most significant question is whether religion will maintain a dynamic tension
with its cultural environment or, as in the case of Niebuhr's two extreme motifs, either abrogate or avoid this
necessary dialectic. In response to rapid change, religion
all too often finds itself unable to cope with modern developments and opts for either a tortoiselike withdrawal
into its own hard shell or amoebalike dislocations that defy
its own inherent character.

From a cogently argued sociological perspective, Robert
Bellah contends that religion is least adaptable to progress
when there is either too close a fusion between religious
symbolism and the actual world, or too great a disjunction
between them.[6] By way of contrast, progress is most likely
to take place in a situation where religious ideals are in
tension with an empirical reality accepted as a meaningful
and valid sphere of action.[7] Niebuhr's three categories of
dialectical tension between religion and cultural society
are subsumed by Bellah under the rubric of "creative tension" between religious ideals and the world. The remaining options are the fusion of the two or their disjunction.

Religion in creative tension with a cultural society provides a kind of collective heritage of "reality testing" with stable points of reference in times of transience.[8] While this limiting function of religion may inhibit necessary change, at its best it provides a needed backdrop for the identity crisis that transitional societies such as those of Asia are experiencing, or, for that matter, the identity crisis of our own culture. The profundity of the social alienation felt by different segments of American society has created a collective soul-searching in which traditional presuppositions and values are being called into question. In the light of this crisis the response of religion in America has been greatly diverse. Such developments as new forms and patterns of church life, the theological revolution staged by the "secular" or "radical" theologians, and the intellectual ferment associated with such conclaves as Vatican II point to the involvement of religion in the West with problems spawned by modernity and change.

In Asia and in the West the role being played by religion in the current crisis of identity is, however, problematical. A creative tension between religious ideals and sociocultural change that provides both continuity and innovation is all too often singularly lacking. Instead we often find attempts to vindicate religion in the face of change or the synthetic adjustment of the religious system to new social conditions. Neither of these two responses (disjunction or fusion) can be adequate. The kind of dialectic called for has been artfully articulated by an Asian scholar of religion as follows:

Essentially, for each of the religions in our societies, the problem is to relate itself to the great and pressing revolution of our time— the effort to abolish poverty, ignorance, and indignity; the striving for a better life on this earth; the emergence of a new social structure; and the continuous presence of change—in

terms other than regret or wistfulness, fear, grudging
acceptance, self-justification, or militant fundamental
rejection.[9]

When everything has been said and done, it is
only a new religious impulse from within the religion
concerned that can give the process of reorientation
and redirection a new and real vitality. . . . It is
. . . only through the spiritual agony engendered by
facing the crises of the times and through reaching
from the depths of one's own religious experience
that it becomes possible to reaffirm and restate one's
religion's essential relationship with society and re-
integrate the moral forces impelling the convulsive
changes of our time into the living center of one's
religion. Then it is possible, to meet the "necessity
of reinterpreting the unalterable, fundamental positions, without which a religion loses its self identity"
and to achieve the "re-directing and re-inspiring of
the religious will." [10]

The times in which we live demand that the historic
religions find within themselves the strength of reorientation and the wisdom of genuine reformation. Certain aspects of Buddhism in Southeast Asia indicate there is some
hope that such revitalization will take place. The following
chapters, while largely descriptive, will attempt to make
an affirmative case for the role of Buddhism present and
future, not only in Asia but also in the West. We acknowledge that our position is biased toward a positive view of
Buddhism's contribution toward "the coming world civili-
zation(s)," but we believe the bias not to be wholly un-
warranted.

D. K. S.

Oberlin College

I

BUDDHISM AND ASIA

Kandy was the last capital of the Sinhalese kings and is still the religious center of Ceylon. It is a beautiful but rather sleepy town—except in July and August during the Kandy Perahera, the largest religious festival in Kandy. There are few cars in Kandy. Import restrictions make it nearly prohibitive to bring a car into the country. Sometimes butter is difficult to find, as is the sweetened condensed milk so many Ceylonese use in their afternoon tea. High tea at one of the old plantation homes remains an experience to be relished.

Ceylonese trains are punctual, and with Ceylon's independence, first-class compartments were eliminated. The journey from Kandy to Anuradhapura, the ancient capital of Ceylon, takes several hours. On the way one passes many fields that have been cleared for rice cultivation, but planting has been slow. The economy is still largely dependent on tea exports. How long will economic diversification take? So many important issues of national development get lost in politics.

In December, 1968, I returned to Bangkok, Thailand, after an absence of eight years. With the anticipation of all homecomings, I looked for familiar landmarks. What a rude shock! The narrow road that wound through rice paddies and past temples had been replaced by a modern superhighway. The air-conditioned airport car delivered its passengers to a series of magnificent, modern hotels, making its way through streets congested with newly imported, Japanese cars. Few of the sights looked familiar. The old canal and the halting trolley on the street where I had lived had made way for a four-lane street. Everywhere the noise of construction booms. Tourists and American servicemen are prominent. It is said that Thai university students visit the Petburi Road club-and-bar district to get an idea of what America is really like.

The Zengakuren students of Doshisha University in Kyoto, Japan, were snaking their way through the streets around the university. They had trained for this exercise the day before on the grounds of the old Imperial Palace across the street. They ran past the Zen temple next to the university, chanting their dislike of the Mutual Security Pact between Japan and the United States. The striking students had closed down the school, as they had several times that spring and summer over a variety of issues including their disapproval of the nominations for the university presidency. Many parents say they cannot understand their college-age children and bemoan what they consider to be their lack of respect.

These three snapshots of contemporary Asia provide an impression of the sorts of changes occurring in the countries of Ceylon, Thailand, and Japan. There are vast differences among them, making it virtually impossible to generalize about religion and change in Asia. In Southeast Asia, nevertheless, there are similar types of problems accompanying trends of modernization, industrialization, postcolonial nationalism, and the response to Western values and culture. The role of religion in this transitional period will be crucial, since religious identification offers virtually the only translocal means of personal and social identity.[1] Whether Buddhism will be able to reform itself and thereby maintain a creative tension with its cultural society remains to be seen. Significant changes are occurring within Buddhism, but it is not entirely clear whether these responses might either disjoin Buddhism from or submerge it with its newly developing contextual matrix.

THERAVĀDA[2] BUDDHISM: A HISTORICAL PERSPECTIVE

Buddhism arose in Northern India in the sixth century B.C. As is the case with the historical religions of Christianity and Islam, its founding focused on a charismatic leader whose genius crystallized a number of forces ripe for synthesis. Tradition acknowledges this founder to be Siddhartha Gotama. According to the Buddhist mythological and legendary accounts, he was born in a miraculous manner at Lumbinī near the modern borders of Nepal and India. The future Buddha ("the Enlightened One") is depicted as the son of the ruler of the Sakya clan, although scholars generally agree that the claims made for his royal parentage are exaggerated. The legends do, however, afford a graphic depiction of the significance of the Buddha's quest for Truth. His decision to adopt the path of a homeless wanderer demanded that he renounce the assured pleasures and satisfactions of the householder life and the promise of political power and authority. Siddhartha's decision paralleled a later conquest of the forces of the sensate world personified by the demon Mara. The story of the Buddha's temptation by the Hosts of Mara prior to his enlightenment is typologically not unlike the temptation of Jesus by Satan. Indeed, in the view of Joseph Campbell, the account of the Buddha's preparation for and attainment of enlightenment fits the classical initiation formula of the hero-god monomyth—the pattern of separation, initiation, return.[3]

The Buddha was the focal point of the development of a new historical religion, but his teachings were not entirely unique. No historic religion simply appears *de novo*, and Buddhism is, as are Christianity and Islam, peculiarly indebted to another great tradition—in this case Brahmanism. Buddhism also appropriated maturing ethical concerns which, by the sixth century, were beginning to challenge the supremacy of the ritualistic and sacrificial preoccupations of the Brahmanic priesthood. In particular it adapted the theory of moral causality, or the Law of Kamma, which underscored the responsibility of each individual for his own actions. Accompanying the Law of Kamma, Buddhism also accepted the notion of rebirth or transmigration (*saṁsāra*), thereby providing both the soteriological dimension of a future reward for meritorious acts and a program for understanding and explaining the causal factors of habituated action. *Kamma* and *saṁsāra*, therefore, furnished early Buddhism not with a deterministic format but, rather, with a schema by which moral and ethical self-improvement could be programmed with predictable consequences.

Many other aspects of Buddhist thought can be traced to origins within the cultural and religious milieu in which early Buddhism developed. Buddhist cosmology, for example, centered about a cosmic mountain (Mt. Meru), an *axis mundi* surrounded by thirty-one spheres, which is reminiscent of Brahmanic thought. Woven into the cosmological design were traditional heavens and the gods who occupied them. Yet, it would be erroneous to depict early Buddhism as merely appropriative and not innovative. The concepts of *kamma* and *saṁsāra* as well as various cosmological notions received modifications, not to mention the new elements found in the early Buddhist doctrine, or Dhamma. Buddhism modified not only the teachings of its predecessors but also many of their practices, including the emphasis on sacrifice and the exclusiveness of the priestly caste. Although the case can be overstated, it is not totally unfounded to depict early Buddhism as a religion of social and religious change. The Buddha objected to religious practices no longer relevant to a changing social environment and modified ideas not pertinent to newly evolving views of man and the world. Early Buddhism, it may be argued, was a unique religious movement within a pluralistic religiosocial milieu and functioned as a catalyst for spiritual renewal.

Within the forty-five-year career of the Buddha and probably for more than the first century of its existence the fledgling Buddhist movement was not highly organized. It centered about a celibate group of wandering truth seekers and teachers and shared much in common with other mendicant groups in Northern India in the sixth century B.C.[4] Its ideals were individualistic and eremitic. In Buddhist countries even today the model of the homeless monk (bhikkhu) "wandering like the lonely rhinoceros" is highly revered. One of the earliest Buddhist texts expresses the ideal in these poetic terms:

> Crave not for tastes, but free of greed,
> Moving with measured step from house

> To house, support of none, none's thrall,
>   Fare lonely as rhinoceros.
>
> Free everywhere, at odds with none,
>   And well content with this and that:
> Enduring dangers undismayed
>   Fare lonely as rhinoceros.[5]

It is interesting to speculate that this tradition of homeless
wanderers did not grow out of the Brahmanic institutions
of early Hinduism but, rather, presents a picture not unlike the peripatetic Sophists of ancient Greece or the wandering Confucian literati who arose to meet the needs of
a new age— in the opinion of Karl Jaspers, the "axial age"
of world civilization.

The early Buddhist community sought to establish an
environment where, on the one hand, spiritual Truth could
be realized in a distinctive manner, but, on the other, from
which the teachings of the Buddha or Buddha Dhamma
could be propagated among other men) This twofold purpose naturally meant that the Buddhist Sangha (monastic
order) was not merely a group of recluses who shunned
the world of the householder for its own sake. It was,
rather, (a community that sought a Middle Way between
the excesses of luxuriousness and deprivation) The moder-
ation of the Buddhist way is rooted in a legend from the
enlightenment quest of the Buddha himself, who, after
undergoing extreme, ascetic practices to a point near death,
realized that physical austerities must be subordinated to
the aim of the realization of Truth.

The eremitic nature of the Buddha's followers gradually
changed. This change was brought about in part by the
growing popularity of Buddhism. As the number of bhikkhus increased, it simply became necessary to provide for

larger groups of followers. The change was also occasioned by the practice that mendicant groups had developed of coming together in some sort of communal situation during the monsoon rains. These "rain retreats" (*vassa*), as they were called, provided opportunity to rehearse the growing formulations of the Buddha's teachings, that bond which allied his followers, but it also became necessary to formulate rules for communal living to which the bhikkhus bound themselves. These rules, known as the *paṭimokkha*, must originally have been largely practical in nature. Gradually, however, they assumed a confessional form and were repeated fortnightly, a practice continued in Theravāda Buddhist countries today. The *paṭimokkha*, in time, came to be encased in a larger body of procedural and disciplinary materials known as the *vinaya*. Within five hundred years, the traditions of doctrine and discipline handed down orally were written on palm leaf texts organized into three broad categories, or "baskets" (*tipitaka*) referred to as the dialogues (*sutta*), the discipline (*vinaya*), and the higher doctrine (*abhidhamma*).

During the formative period of Buddhism in India, a relatively dynamic situation must have prevailed in the relationships between monk and layman. The Pāli texts support such a contention. Many of the stereotyped teaching situations depicted in the dialogue (*sutta*) texts are between the Buddha or one of his followers and laymen. Furthermore, it is apparent that some of the early rain retreat centers (*āvāsa*) were lands donated by the wealthy gentry. That early Buddhism entered into a dynamic interaction with its sociocultural matrix is also supported by evidence from the earliest Buddhist sites in India at Sanchi and Bharhut. Here are found large, dome-shaped reliquaries, or stupas, to which tens of thousands of pilgrims must

have found their way to perform pious acts of merit even
as they do today in Theravāda countries. In addition, the
bas-reliefs carved in the gate pillars depict a variety of
scenes and motifs that testify to the almost earthy natural-
ism of the Buddhism flourishing in India two hundred
years after the death of its founder.

Early Buddhism also had a strong ethical appeal, as is
evidenced by the Rock Edicts of King Aśoka, the third
century B.C. ruler of the Maurya Dynasty. Aśoka was the
most important Buddhist monarch in India and under his
authority much of India came under the influence of Buddhism. According to legend, Aśoka was converted by Buddhist teachings from a sword-wielding conqueror into a
welfare-oriented, benevolent monarch. In contemporary
Theravāda countries, Aśoka is still revered as the exemplary
model of the ideal Buddhist ruler (*cakkavattin*), whose
principal function is to exercise the spiritual power of the
Buddha through humanitarian rule in the mundane realm.
Aśoka's Dhamma, or Buddhist teaching, is almost star-
tling in its plainness: "One should obey one's father and
mother. One should respect the supreme value and sa-
credness of life. One should speak the truth. One should
practice these virtues of Dharma. In the same way, pupils
should honor their teachers, and in families one should
behave with fitting courtesy to relatives. This is the traditional rule of Dharma, and it is conducive to long life.
Men should act according to it." [6] Some Western scholars
have noted that Aśoka's teachings seem strangely incon-
sistent with the world-denying tendencies they perceive in
classical Theravāda doctrine. The point they overlook is
that Aśoka's Buddhism was probably closer to the popular
tradition than to classical teachings of monastic Buddhism.
We should ask ourselves what the church fathers might

have thought of the religion of Constantine or, for that matter, what they would have had to say about the religion of an American President!

With the establishment of permanent monastic institutions and a scholastic tradition, some of the earlier dynamic of Buddhism was sacrificed, especially in those parts of India and Ceylon where the Pāli or Theravāda tradition of Buddhism predominated. Some of the great Buddhist monastic universities such as Nālandā were important centers of learning up to the tenth century A.D., and the stories surrounding the Buddhist monarchs of Ceylon point to the fact that Buddhism continued to exert a vital role in certain parts of South Asia for several centuries. Nevertheless, in its competition with other philosophical schools and religious sects, the orthodox Theravāda tradition tended to become unduly dominated by scholastic minutiae and overly preoccupied with issues that the Buddha would have claimed did "not tend toward edification." The Abhidhamma tradition is a reflection of this scholastic preoccupation, and some of the detailed speculation about psychological and cosmological constructs in the Abhidhamma texts remind one of such medieval theological problems as the number of souls required to fill the precincts of heaven! Yet, it would be unfair to the Theravāda tradition to caricature its history in such a fashion. Much of the essential insight of early Buddhism was retained and has continued to express itself in the Buddhism of the Theravāda countries of Southeast Asia.

THERAVĀDA BUDDHISM: A DOCTRINAL PERSPECTIVE

The religion of the classical Theravāda tradition as it was to be preserved in South India and Ceylon and from

there to spread to Southeast Asia, where it became the
state religion in Burma, Thailand, Cambodia, and Laos, is
rooted in the perception of the transient and evanescent
nature of the mundane world. Time is fleeting. Nothing
is permanent. Not only is there constant change within
the observable natural environment; man, in particular, is
subject to the whims of his physical body, the volatility of
his feelings, and the fickleness of his intentions. He has no
peace. He is as a small raft tossed to and fro by the seas of
change.

The transient nature of the mundane world is a given,
but unlike Chinese Taoism, Indian Buddhism does not
see the inevitability of movement in terms of harmony and
goodness. Change is not understood as profound and accepted as the natural pattern of life; rather, it is to be
transcended. The Theravādin sees change as dangerous because he believes that the ordinary man is unable to accept
it and act in terms of it. Man suffers (*dukkha*) because,
even though he and his world are in a continuous state of
flux, he acts as though this were not the case. He seeks a
permanent satisfaction from material wealth which in the
twinkling of an eye may be lost and he strives to maintain
the physical beauty of youth which inevitably passes away
with time. Above all, deep in the recesses of human consciousness is the notion of a Self, an Ego, or a Soul, which
is dimly perceived to be the inherent subject of all human
activity. The idea of Self (*atta*) is the primary cause of
man's suffering. It is the source of his attachment to a
ceaseless number of things and brings about the distinctions of "I" and "mine" when in reality such distinctions
do not exist. The point is illustrated by an oft-quoted dialogue between the Buddhist monk, Nāgasena, and Milinda
or Menander, ruler of the Indo-Greek state of Bactria in

the second century B.C. In the dialogue, Milinda asks
Nāgasena what he is called and he replies, "Nāgasena
. . . but . . . it is, nevertheless, your majesty, but a way
of counting, a term, an appellation, a convenient designa-
tion, a mere name, this Nāgasena; for there is no Ego here
to be found." [7] He goes on to prove this claim to the evi-
dent satisfaction of the king by pointing out that nothing
he could designate such as his body or feelings could be
properly called Nāgasena; however, at the same time, he
could not be something besides bodily "form, sensation,
perception, the predispositions and consciousness," hence,
"verily . . . Nāgasena is a mere empty sound. What Nāgasena is there here? Bhante (Revered Lord), you speak
a falsehood, a lie: there is no Nāgasena." [8]

The famous "no-soul" (anatta) doctrine of classical
Theravāda Buddhism is essentially a part of the teachings
of universal impermanence (anicca) and suffering (dukkha). These three concepts taken together are referred to
as the Three Signs (ti-lakkhaṇa), or characteristics, of existence. They point to reality as an atomistic, ongoing process in which nothing in life is free from the conditions of
its environment. Consequently, everything in the mundane
world is relative. All existent entities are part of a cyclical
process of causal becoming in which the parts are both
conditioned and conditioning. This cyclical process has
been described by the Theravādins in the formula of Dependent Origination (paṭicca-samuppāda).[9] Whereas in its
present twelve-stage form it roots the process of becoming
in ignorance (avijjā), the main point seems to be that any
particular step is relative to or conditioned by any other
step in the formula. The paṭicca-samuppāda is a paradigm
illustrating the fact that any particular aspect of existence
is conditioned by an interconnecting web of psychological

and cosmological processes many of which are beyond our direct and immediate observation.

On the surface the Three Signs and what they state about the relative and conditioned nature of the world imply an attitude of negativism and pessimism. Indeed, certain Western scholars have interpreted Buddhism in this way. They insist that the Theravāda tradition takes life to be illusory or unreal and therefore rejects the concept of meaningful activity in the world. Such an interpretation is a distortion of Theravāda teaching. Buddhism claims, rather, that existence is unreal or illusory only to the extent that man himself misunderstands it. This misunderstanding is based upon the erroneous impression that the world surrounding us has a stability it does not really possess. Our senses tell us that the table on which we are writing today will be the same tomorrow, next week, and the following year. Our affections for those we love assume a permanence of human relationships which, in fact, does not exist. Because of these misimpressions we become attached to things that do not possess the inherent nature we attribute to them. The fundamental problem rests with sensory attachments. If these attachments and the resultant perceptual distortions can be overcome, then there is some hope that a true understanding of the nature of things can be reached.

The above characterization of Theravāda teachings underlines the fact that Buddhism's "negative" teachings of no-soul or no-self (*anatta*) and the noneternal nature (*anicca*) of the mundane world are not really negative but an empirical assessment of the true nature of things. The negative implications of these teachings have the positive intention of pointing men toward a true understanding of themselves and their environment. Such understanding is fundamentally soteriological in nature. Buddhism, as well as Christianity and the other great historical religions, is ultimately soteriological in nature. These religions direct men toward a transformed existence, a "new being." In Buddhism this transformed existence is indicated by the term "Nibbāna," or "Nirvāṇa." Above all, it points to a state of being in which the attachments to self-oriented activity productive of hatred, greed, and delusion are overcome. It is a state in which desires (taṇhā) have been transformed, for without that transformation the senses will continue to misguide and misinform man's quest for enlightened existence.

The Buddhist goal of Nibbāna is not clearly defined in the Pāli texts and for this reason has given rise to a variety of interpretations. Some scholars have rendered it as a state of personal annihilation, while others have taken it to represent a transcendent state of bliss. It must be said, in the last analysis, that Nibbāna, as the Ultimately Real, is beyond conceptualization. As Edward Conze puts it: "Nirvana is 'unthinkable' or 'unconceivable' if only because there is nothing general about it, and everyone must experience it personally for himself; because there is nothing in the world even remotely like it, and because reasoning (tarka) cannot get anywhere near it. All conceptions of Nirvana are misconceptions."[10] That the realization of the goal of Buddhism is through a personal quest has been one of its most salient characteristics. Consequently there has been a strong emphasis throughout the history of Buddhism on the way (magga) to salvation. Traditionally this way has been expressed through the formula of the Noble Eightfold Path. It is summarized as right views, right intention, right speech, right action, right livelihood, right effort, right mindfulness, right concentration. These eight categories can be divided roughly into three classifications: virtuous action or morality, concentration or meditation, and saving knowledge or wisdom. In one sense the steps of the way are overlapping concentric circles rather than successive stages; however, they also suppose that the way to Nibbāna is a progressive development that begins with a foundation of moral action and culminates in the realization of transcendent wisdom.

The Buddhist path to salvation is one of both physical and mental discipline. Yet, unlike certain Yoga practices, the discipline of the Buddhist way is never an end in itself. Buddhist meditation does not aim at control but at liberation. It is a process in which the development of awareness and insight are central. Trance states and supernatural powers may, indeed, be part of the consequences of meditation but they are incidental to its goal. Buddhist meditation aims at knowing the Really Real through experience. It is a way to appropriate in a total fashion what has been known only by discursive reason. In a sense, therefore, the wisdom acquired through meditation is not totally unlike the Christian notion of faith. But, unlike the Christian understanding of faith, the salvation goal is strictly the result of one's own effort. By the program of the Buddhist way, one arrives at that perfect freedom where, by the power of detachment, one is no longer subject to the bondage of the mundane world. Through true understanding, the misconceptions fostered by the senses are overcome and one acquires the condition of sainthood, namely, the power to be in the world but not of it.

Because Theravāda Buddhism developed within the confines of the monastery, its traditions tended to become more scholastic and, perhaps, more sterile. The basic teachings of the early tradition, which included the three characteristics of existence (*dukkha, anicca, anatta*) and the even more widely known formulas of the Four Noble Truths and the Eightfold Path, gradually evolved into highly elaborated and complex schemes of existence.[11] Yet, even Theravāda scholasticism was never completely divorced from the "middle way" nature of Buddhism. The monastic forms of Buddhism did not develop in isolation from their cultural contexts; consequently, both Buddhism's ultimate, "otherworldly" ideal of Nibbāna and its ethical teachings for the layman and popular forms of devotion were influential in forming the cultural societies of Ceylon, Burma, Thailand, Cambodia, and Laos. Just as Mahāyāna forms of Buddhism mutually influenced and were influenced by Taoism, Confucianism, and archaic forms of religion and magic in China and Japan, Theravāda Buddhism competed with and absorbed Hindu deities in Ceylon and *nat* and *phi* spirits in Burma and Thailand. Buddhism, furthermore, was used by rulers in most of these Southeast Asian countries to help establish political and social unity. The identity of a Burman or a Thai, for instance, is so conditioned by Buddhism that his nationality almost assumes he is a Buddhist.

Buddhism has been a determinative factor in the Asian personal and social consciousness for two thousand years. It has contributed essentially to attitudes of life and death; inspired the architecture and splendor of the ancient capitals of Polonnāruwa, Pagan, Sukhōthai, and Angkor Thom; articulated theories of governance according to the pattern of the ideal Buddhist world ruler (*cakkavattin*); appropriated responsibility for the maintenance of continuity at the crisis times of life (*rites de passage*); influenced decisively such great philosophies of life as Hinduism, Taoism, and Confucianism; continues to be in many Asian coun-

tries the major social institution outside of the family; and
has been largely responsible for articulating both the
ultimate and proximate goals of individuals and societies.
In the modern period, the traditional role of Buddhism
has been challenged by Western political theories and
social and religious values, modern technology, and the
many tensions accompanying modernization and industrialization. Although Buddhism has always been involved
in its cultural societies, its monastic emphasis, the nature
of its ultimate goal, and the path to it have tended to give
it an otherworldly ethos. The major problem of religion
and change, from the standpoint of the Buddhist tradition
itself, is for religion to be able to sustain a creative tension
with its cultural society, to maintain the perspective to
discern the difference between valid and invalid commit-
ments and goals, and to maintain the authority to be able
to challenge those forces directing the processes of change.
Without discernment Buddhism will be seduced into jus-
tifying those who wish to bring about change simply on
their own terms, and without authority it will be endan-
gered of retreating into a chrysalis of dogmatic and irrelevant self-righteousness. We do not mean to imply that
Buddhism has nothing within its tradition with which to
cope with the demands of modernity. On the contrary, its
teachings about the inevitability of change and the necessary and consequential responsibility of all human actions
(*kamma*) provide two important perspectives on the
transition many Asian societies are making today. Nevertheless, to influence change, Buddhism itself must change.
It cannot simply affirm old teachings in outmoded forms.
To do so would not only divorce Buddhism from playing a
much-needed role in the process of modernization but
would deny it the kind of reformation it, itself, needs. The

problem of religion and change, as stated in the Introduction, pertains basically to the dialectic between religion and its cultural society. In the relationship of creative tension not only is a culture influenced by religion, but, in turn, religion is influenced by its cultural society. This creative tension must exist in both Asian and Western cultural contexts if religion is to play a dynamic role in this period of transition and change.

II

BUDDHISM AND NATIONALISM

One of the strongest impressions that a person has of contemporary Asia is a climate of intense national feeling despite the significant degree of communalism in such countries as Ceylon and Burma. This nationalism stems in large part from a continuing response to the long period of colonial domination by the Portuguese, Dutch, British, and French. In Ceylon, for example, the Portuguese arrived in the sixteenth century, only to be succeeded by the Dutch in the seventeenth and the British in the nineteenth, who were also ruling at the same time in India and Burma. Many of the educated elite of these former colonial countries, while they admire Western technology and are indebted to Western political and economic theories, are suspicious of Western values and life-styles. They are drawn, as it were, into a love-hate relationship with their former "parent." And, as often happens in families, many Asian nations are in one stage or another of the sort of identity crisis that leads to a seeming rejection of the parent. It has involved breaking many ties with former dominant Western powers and searching for a new national identity. There is suspicion of any great power exercising excessive influence over them—especially, at present, the United States. This suspicion is derived from the predominating role the U.S. is playing in Vietnam, Thailand, and Laos, as well as the nature of our foreign-aid support, which has been, as in the case of Ceylon, seemingly contingent on an anti-Communist/pro-United States stance. America has a large store of goodwill remaining in Asia; however, we need to be extraordinarily sensitive to the fact that, in the minds of certain of the educated elite, any massive Western presence runs the risk of compromising the independence of these countries. (One might add that there is a similar fear of mainland China.) Our task in this chapter, however, is not to discuss Asian nationalism or America's role in Asia but the problem of Buddhism and nationalism. First some of the historic connections between Buddhism and nationalism in Southeast Asia will be mentioned, and then the contemporary scene will be studied under three categories: the charismatic Buddhist political leader, the role of the Sangha (monastic order), and the development of Buddhist lay movements of an overt or covert political nature.

BUDDHISM AND NATIONALISM: A HISTORICAL PERSPECTIVE

The history of Buddhism throughout much of Asia has been intimately bound up with national unity. Indeed, as was the case with such rulers as Devānampiyatissa of Ceylon (third century B.C.), King Anawratha in Burma (eleventh century A.D.), and Jayavaram VII of the Khmers (thirteenth century A.D.), Buddhism assisted in unifying the country under the authority of one rule. The traditional relationship between Buddhist institutions and secular rulers was, in general, one of interdependency. It was interdependent in the sense that Buddhist kings guaranteed the protection and promotion of Buddhism in exchange for the sanction and recognition of the Sangha. Richard Gard contends that this situation prevailed in Ceylon and Southeast Asia until the advent of colonialism, in Central Asia prior to the arrival of Islam, in Mongolia and Tibet until the Communist revolution, and in premodern China, Japan, and Korea, except in periods and areas where Confucian, Taoist, or Shinto beliefs predominated.[1] On the other hand, Buddhism has also borne a relationship of dependency vis à vis secular jurisdiction. Buddhist kings often held authority over the Sangha as well as the state. This situation still formally prevails in Thailand, where the king appoints the Sangharājā, or head of the Buddhist order. Even though Buddhist institutions gained political influence as their prestige and wealth increased, they seldom altered the sociopolitical structure of the nation.[2] On occasion a Buddhist monk rose to some political prominence but, likely as not, it was to persuade a ruler to take action in the religious sphere, such as reforming the Sangha or ostracizing a group of heretical monks. Exceptions to this kind of pattern in Sangha-state relationships occurred at times of weak secular authority or of foreign intervention. Then monks exerted a more overt political role. Burma posed just such a situation in the 1920's.[3] Vietnam does today. Because of the historic role that Buddhism has played in the development of a sense of national identity, as well as the long-standing, interactive relationship between Sangha and state, the present picture of Buddhist political involvement should not be regarded as a new religion, "a sort of embodiment of the national ideologies and aspirations of present-day Asians with the trappings of traditional Buddhist vocabulary and symbols." [4] Rather,

it would be more accurate to say "that socio-economic and
political developments in recent decades have greatly aided
Buddhism in rediscovering its own potentialities and
genius, buried and forgotten" under colonial regimes.[5]

Despite its seemingly otherworldly goal of Nibbāna and
lack of a full-blown social or political philosophy, Buddhism has contributed to political thought and principles
of politicosocial conduct; and monks have rendered administrative and diplomatic assistance.[6] Pāli texts mention a
social-compact theory of society and a governmental-con-
tract theory of kingship. The contractual theory of kingship
gradually developed into the notion of the king as the
ideal Buddhist universal ruler (cakkavattin) who governs
through his personal merit for the well-being and security
of the individual and society. The paradigmatic historical
figure fulfilling this role was Aśoka, ruler of the Maurya
Dynasty in Northern India in the third century B.C., who
is accredited with numerous acts of social and Buddhist
welfare, including the commissioning of Buddhist missions to many parts of Asia. Other Buddhist rulers are similarly revered within particular national histories. For example, Dutthagāmani of Ceylon is considered to be the
savior of Buddhism from the Hindu Tamils in the first century B.C., and Jayavaram VII, builder of Angkor Thom,
was revered both as a Buddhist bodhisatta ("wisdom-being") as well as a Hindu God-king.

The histories of Buddhism in Ceylon and each of the
Southeast Asian countries are distinctive. Yet, with the
exception of Vietnam, Theravāda Buddhism of the Sinhalese variety became the orthodox state religion in all of
them. To reach this status it competed successfully with
Brahmanic Hinduism, Mahāyāna sects, and indigenous
cults, partially assimilating aspects of them. Consequently,
while there was a certain universal kinship under the

Buddhist Dhamma, or doctrine, the Theravāda Buddhism
of each country developed along distinctly national lines.
Unlike the universalism of Islam with a holy city, Mecca,
or the caste communalism of Hinduism, Theravāda Buddhism in Southeast Asia was defined more in terms of
national identification. As a result, in the postcolonial
period, Buddhism has played an exceptionally significant
political role, particularly in Ceylon, Burma, and Vietnam.
Immediately prior to and following independence in both
Ceylon and Burma, the political role of the Sangha waned.
In the face of the frustrations and lack of progress of the
earlier years of nationhood, however, Buddhism as a potential political ideology, as well as the political power of the
Sangha, increased in importance. In both Burma and
Ceylon a strong Buddhist political leader emerged. And,
as it turned out, the exploitation of Buddhism by these
leaders eventually resulted in their demise. The Vietnamese situation offers a different pattern. It was the political pressure brought to bear on the Diem regime in
1963 by the Buddhists that eventuated in its downfall.
That pressure continued to be exerted on Thieu and Ky.
It may well be that of all the Southeast Asian countries
South Vietnam will be the one where Buddhism plays the
weightiest role in establishing political stability. In the
other Buddhist countries of Southeast Asia as well, however, national development will hinge partially on the nature of the contribution made by Buddhism.

CHARISMATIC BUDDHIST POLITICAL LEADERS:
U NU, S.W.R.D. BANDARANAIKE, NORODOM SIHANOUK

Traditionally, the most critical integrating forces in
Asian society have been the monarchy and Buddhism, a

situation that still holds true in Thailand today. The king was looked upon as the protector of the Sāsana;[7] he did battle for it, built edifices to house it, called councils to purify it, enforced its monastic discipline (*vinaya*), and, in some cases, is reputed to have been exceptionally devout and scholarly. In theory the king was considered as either a divine incarnation (Java, ancient Cambodia) or an exceptionally holy man, a *cakkavattin* (Burma, Thailand), on the basis of previously accumulated good *kamma*.[8] His rule was essential to the maintenance of a sacred order cosmologically conceived, as evidenced by regalia, state ceremonies, and architecture. He was a charismatic leader by virtue of his office and, on occasion, reinforced by a personal charisma as well (e.g., King Mongkut of Siam). With the disruption of traditional Asian society in the nineteenth and twentieth centuries, the role of the Buddhist monarch was eclipsed. Remnants of these old cultural traditions still remain in Cambodia, Laos, and Thailand. Indeed, during the past decade in Thailand, there has been a concerted effort on the part of the government to restore some of the ancient, royal rituals dispensed with after the 1932 coup d'état which toppled the absolute monarchy. Beyond that, however, there have been two outstanding politicians who, within a democratic-parliamentary framework, have captured something of the personal charisma of the ancient conception of the Buddhist monarch as the righteous protector of the faith. In both cases, in fact, the question of restoring Buddhism to its rightful place as the *de jure* state religion was seriously considered. Of these political leaders, the best known in the West is U Nu, former prime minister of Burma.

The political career of U Nu ("Mr. Tender") provides the focal point for the history of the Burmese independence movement, which began in the first decades of the twentieth century.[9] At the outset Buddhism provided the impetus for Burmese nationalism. As John F. Cady observes:

> The primary role played by religious considerations in the emergence of naissant Burmese nationalism can be attributed to the fact that religion afforded the only universally acceptable symbol to represent an accumulation of grievances, economic, social and psychological, which were as yet for the most part inarticulate and incapable of direct political exploitation.[10]

The first issue of consequence was the "no footwear" controversy of 1918 brought to a head by politically conscious members of the Young Men's Buddhist Association (Y.M.B.A.). They argued that Europeans in consonance with Burmese custom should be prohibited from wearing shoes in all pagoda premises. For the next decade the nationalist cause was led primarily by the General Council of Burmese Associations and politically active monks such as U Ottama and U Wisara. This basically Buddhist-inspired movement was replaced in the period of the '30s to the end of World War II by more secularly oriented organizations such as the Thakins, led by General Aung San, and the Anti-Fascist People's Freedom League (A.F.P.F.L.), which spawned such leaders as U Nu and General Ne Win. When Aung San was assassinated on the eve of the declaration of Burmese independence (January 4, 1948), U Nu was called upon to form the new government. Although the A.F.P.F.L. party had been established on the principle of religious neutrality, Buddhism became, under the leadership of U Nu, the *sine qua non* of its political program.

U Nu conceived of Buddhism as providing the basic answer to Burma's many postindependence problems. Although by the time he became prime minister his earlier identification of Buddhism with Marxism had been cast aside, he consistently espoused a philosophy of Buddhist socialism. In essence it was based on the theory that a national community could be constructed only if the individual members were able to overcome their own self-acquisitive interests. Material things such as property are "meant not to be saved, not for gains nor comfort. It is to be used by men to meet their needs in respect of clothing, food, habitation in their journey towards Nirvana." [11] Property and class distinctions have been responsible for oppression and warfare. In the spirit of Buddhist self-abnegation they should be transcended for the good of the larger community. In such fashion, U Nu attempted to speak as the Buddhist rulers of old whose charisma was associated with a superior knowledge about the causality of deliverance from suffering (dukkha). Only, in this case, the ruler's soteriological insight had been transmuted into the charismatic statesman's superior knowledge of the causality of social reform.[12]

The genius of U Nu was his ability to bridge tradition and modernity and to speak in terms the majority of the Buddhist populace could understand while at the same time infusing them with the concepts of Western political ideology. He had the uncanny ability to present innovations as elaborations of orthodoxy, to support and encourage change without jeopardizing the support of the masses. Utilizing the Buddhist eschatological notion of the ideal state of the perfect Buddhist ruler (cakkavattin), he preached a socialistic doctrine of a classless society without want in which all members would strive for moral and

mental perfection in order to overcome the constant round
of rebirths (saṁsāra). To attain this end the disciplines of
Buddhism, especially meditation, were held up as the
means by which an earthly Nibbāna could be achieved.

Some of Nu's opponents have attempted to discredit
him by suggesting that he exploited religion to gain political ends; however, his personal life would belie such a
charge. He rose regularly at four thirty A.M. to spend two
hours in meditation. He entered the monastery over seven
times, and, despite his affection for his family, upheld a
vow of sexual abstinence from 1948 to his death. He wrote
frequently on Buddhism and during a visit to the United
States in 1956 spent much of his time lecturing on the
subject. Regarding programs to stimulate the development
of Buddhism, he created a Buddhist Sāsana Council in
1950 to propagate Buddhism and supervise monks, appointed a minister of religious affairs, and ordered government departments to dismiss civil servants thirty minutes
early if they wished to meditate.[13] At the cost of six million
dollars, he constructed a peace pagoda and large assembly
hall in Rangoon to house the epoch-making Buddhist
Jayanti Synod (1954–1956) and spent considerable sums
to restore Buddhist monuments in Burma.

Far from exploiting Buddhism for political ends, others
have suggested, U Nu helped to bring about his own demise
in 1962 by his overly naïve conviction that religion would
save his country. There are many instances when he evidenced a near magical belief in the efficacy of particular
religious acts. For example, when he took his vow of sexual
abstinence he is reported to have said, "On July 20, 1948,
when the insurrection was causing anxiety, I went into my
prayer room and before the Holy Image took the vow of
absolute purity, making a wish at that time that if I kept
that vow the insurgents would be confounded." [14] He

strongly supported the worship of *nats* (local Burmese spirits or deities) and frequently consulted an astrologer. Donald E. Smith contends that Nu escaped from the hard requirements of political leadership through his many religious activities, and that his continual preoccupation with religious matters robbed him of a rational approach to political, economic, and social problems.[15] Despite such a charge, U Nu's genius for synthesis appears to be the kind of attitude that must characterize the leaders of traditional Asian societies adapting to modernity.

In Ceylon the Buddhist political leader who occupied the place corresponding to U Nu in Burma was S.W.R.D. Bandaranaike.[16] He participated in the first wave of Ceylonese nationalism exemplified by the Ceylon National Congress formed in 1919. He was the leader of the Sinhala Maha Sabha representing Sinhalese and Buddhist interests, the second largest group within the coalition United National Party (U.N.P.) which ruled Ceylon after independence in 1948. In a struggle over party leadership Bandaranaike left the U.N.P. in 1951 to form the Sri Lanka Freedom Party (S.L.F.P.). In 1956 he was swept into the office of prime minister strongly backed by Buddhist and Sinhalese nationalistic sentiment augmented by two important events of the same year—the celebration of the Buddha Jayanti (the twenty-five-hundredth anniversary of the birth of the Buddha) and the publication of a scathing report denouncing the legacy of wrongs suffered by the Sinhalese Buddhists throughout the years of colonialism. As B. H. Farmer cogently remarks, "Bandaranaike's election represented the second wave of nationalism strongly emphasizing Sinhalese and Buddhist interests and directed against anything considered to be 'residual imperialism.'" [17]

Bandaranaike's election was one of the most decisive

turning points in the revival of Buddhism. The revival had
begun during the latter quarter of the nineteenth century
with the activity of some articulate and aggressive bhikkhus and the coalescing support of Henry Steel Olcott, the
American theosophist. It was furthered by the formation
of such lay groups as the Maha Bodhi Society (1891) led
by the Anagarika Dharmapala, a key figure in the resurgence, and in the Young Men's Buddhist Association of
Colombo (1898). The momentum of the revival continued
through a steady increase in Buddhist private schools and
through the organization of the All Ceylon Buddhist
Congress. The latter, especially with the publication of the
Report of the Buddhist Committee of Inquiry referred to
above, and the Lanka Bauddha Mandalaya appointed in
1954 to organize and direct the Buddha Jayanti activities,
helped to create a milieu favorable to Bandaranaike's
victory.

Even though Bandaranaike's opponents insisted he exploited Buddhism largely for political interests, it appears
that he, like U Nu, can be considered an exponent of
Buddhist socialism. But unlike Nu's, Bandaranaike's personal life did not reflect a preoccupying religious orientation. Instead, he supported the idea of adopting Buddhism
as the state religion in order to usher in an era of religio-
democratic socialism.[18] In an address delivered in Kandy at
the inaugural meeting of the World Fellowship of Buddhists in 1950 he expounded his philosophy as follows:

> I believe in democracy because I believe in the Bud-
> dhist doctrine, that a man's worth should be meas-
> ured by his own merit and not some extraneous cir-
> cumstance and also that human freedom is a priceless
> possession. The Buddha preached that ultimate free-
> dom of man when the human mind need not be
> subject even to the will of God, and man was free to

decide for himself what was right or wrong. . . . In economics I consider myself a Socialist, for I cannot reconcile, with the spirit of the doctrine of Maitreya, man-made inequalities that condemn a large section of our fellowmen to poverty, ignorance and disease.[19]

Bandaranaike's justication for both his democratic political beliefs and his socialistic economic philosophy rested in Buddhism. He attempted to espouse a "middle way" political ideology that was neutralist in international policy and uniquely Sinhalese in national policy. His election was greatly indebted to the support lent by those who saw him, not so much as a political leader of great piety, but as one who would restore the interests of the majority Sinhalese-Buddhist population. Not the least of these were the bhikkhus, especially those in rural areas from the Amarapura and Ramanya sects. Predictably, Bandaranaike's election unleashed communalistic feelings which overflowed into the language riots of 1958 and eventuated in his assassination in 1962, masterminded and executed, ironically, by disenchanted monks. Nevertheless, Bandaranaike, in the eyes of many Buddhists, is a national hero and stands with the Anagarika Dharmapala as one of the two great leaders in the modern period who, like the ancient kings, Dutthagāmani and Parākramabāhu I, sought to establish the sway of Buddhism over "lovely Lanka."

In the postcolonial period no other Buddhist political leaders measure up to the stature of U Nu or Bandaranaike, with the possible exception of Prince Norodom Sihanouk of Cambodia. Sihanouk stepped down as the monarch of Cambodia in 1955 in order to be elected by popular ballot. He was seeking to reinforce the legitimacy of his rule already assured among many sectors of the population as a God-king in the image of Jayavarman VII. His political position's indebtedness to Buddhist concepts and values may someday help restore him to power in Cambodia. He has been quoted as saying that his view of equality is not based on Marx or the French Revolution but on the teachings of the Buddha.[20] While traditionalistic in many of his beliefs, including the worship of the *phi* (the Cambodian equivalent of the Burmese *nats*), he sees Buddhism as necessary to the development of Cambodia in terms of both its ideology and the role to be played by the Sangha in the areas of education and community development. He justifies the elevation of Buddhism to be the state religion of the country on the grounds that it will thereby serve as an inspiration to its socialism and teach "all virtues with which a citizen or a nation should adorn themselves for their greatest good." [21]

If effective change is to come about in Asia, it will be engineered by charismatic political leaders with the ability to synthesize the traditions familiar to the populace with political, social, and economic policies favorable to modernization and development. Buddhism alone offers the only translocal tradition with the potential for providing creative general limits within which potent, indigenous ideologies might be fashioned. Despite the failures of U Nu and Bandaranaike and the enigmatic complexities of Sihanouk, their attempts to fashion a unique Buddhist socialism sufficient to meet the needs of their transitional societies are potentially the most positive political means to national integration and development.

THE ROLE OF THE SANGHA IN THE SOCIOPOLITICAL REALM

Because of the war in Vietnam, the problem of the Buddhist monk and politics is vaguely a part of the consciousness of most Americans. We have read numerous reports in a wide variety of sources about monks leading political demonstrations, harboring Viet Cong in their temples, and, most dramatically, burning themselves to death to protest the destruction and bloodshed in their country. Yet, for all the publicity few of us understand the intricacies of this problem.[22]

Although in Vietnam Buddhist monks had participated from time to time in resistance to the French, prior to 1963 Buddhism had played a fairly traditional role in Vietnamese society. It was close to the common man but had limited contacts with modernizing elements in society and lacked the national unity necessary to bring to fruition the sputterings of Buddhist renaissance begun in the 1930's through the formation of a variety of Buddhist associations (e.g., Cochinchina Buddhist Study Society, 1931, and the Buddhist Youth Family Movement, 1940).[23] Composing about 65 percent of the total population, Vietnamese Buddhists are predominantly Mahāyānists of the Chinese Ch'an (Japanese, Zen) type, although there is a sizable Theravāda minority found primarily along the Cambodian border. The high point of Buddhism in Vietnam, especially vis à vis cooperation between the Sangha and the Imperial Court, occurred under the Li Dynasty (A.D. 1009–1225), the golden age of Vietnamese history. For Buddhist leaders such as Thich Tri Quang, that period functions as a reminder of the precedent of Buddhist power in Vietnam.

The year 1963 brought the downfall of the Diem regime. Although the immediate cause was a military coup d'état, perhaps the most important factor in Diem's ouster was the opposition of the Buddhists. Through a series of blunders on the part of the government, an irreparable breach was created with the majority of the Buddhists. The cul

de sac was the nationwide raid against many Buddhist
pagodas by troops in full battlegear engineered by Ngo
Dinh Nhu in August, 1963. With most of the militant
monks jailed or in hiding, the resultant Buddhist opposition was expressed through student demonstrations and
occasional self-immolations, but the way had been paved
for the successful coup of November 1. Even though the
Buddhists had been rendered temporarily impotent due to
the incarceration of so many of their leaders, they emerged
as victors from the crisis.[24]

The new Military Revolutionary Council which assumed political leadership wanted to have the backing of
the Buddhists, so they supported the Vietnamese Buddhist
Reunification Congress held the first of January, 1964.
From this meeting emerged the United Vietnamese Buddhist Church (or United Buddhist Association) under
which there were two important organizations: the Institute for Religious Affairs, which appointed Thich Tri
Quang as secretary general, and the Institute for the
Propagation of the Dharma (Institute for Secular Affairs),
led by Thich Tam Chau with representatives in all provinces and most districts.[25] Other organizations were established, including the Buddhist Chaplains Corps, headed
by Thich Tam Giac. Although there were serious divisions
within this movement, in particular between the more
moderate Thich Tam Chau and the more militant Thich
Tri Quang, the United Buddhist Church offered a degree
of unity for one to two million Buddhists that had not
been known for centuries. In addition to more cooperation
between various Buddhist groups, this united effort also
aimed at making Buddhism a more vital force in public
policy formulation and government programs. Thus, the
Institute for Secular Affairs set up an elaborate program

to organize family units as nuclei for social welfare activities and as spearheads for political agitation and action. The chaplains corps laid plans to sponsor cooperatives to sell food, clothing, and other necessities to soldiers' families at reduced prices and provide dependent housing and medical care for soldiers' families.[26]

More direct political action was taken by influential Buddhist monks after this structure was set up. In particular Thich Tri Quang, from his base of power in Hue, was instrumental in the establishment of People's Councils for National Salvation for the purpose of bringing overt political pressure to bear on General Khanh, the leader of the government. After the take-over by Ky the United Buddhist Association acted to establish a position of power with the new government. In March of 1966 they called for an immediate convention to draw up a constitution, national elections, and the return of General Thi, who had been removed from his position in Hue, to his post. These demands precipitated the Buddhist crisis of 1966. The events of that crisis are complicated but they eventuated in the militant leadership of Thich Tri Quang and his associate, Thich Thien Minh, dominating the actions of the United Buddhist Association. Widespread demonstrations were conducted throughout the country with violent disruptions in Da Nang, Hue, and Saigon. The Buddhists succeeded in forcing the government to hold elections, but, in the opinion of Jerrold Schecter, the militancy of some of the Buddhist leaders alienated the broad mass of Buddhist laymen and destroyed the effectiveness and credibility of the church's leadership.[27] Thich Nhat Hanh disagrees with Schecter's interpretation of the action of the Buddhists in the crisis of 1966. In particular, he sees the political role of the militant Buddhist leaders as one thrust upon them by the circumstances of the situation. In his view the Buddhists offer the most important ingredient to a third force in South Vietnam that could build a truly representative and stable government.[28]

Vietnam offers the most dramatic example of Buddhist monks playing an active role in the game of politics. They have demonstrated their power and, although they are divided, they have proved their effectiveness. If called upon, they can line the streets of Saigon with Buddha altars or sway a crowd with politicoreligious oratory. Yet, the militant monk at the barricades will not, in the long run, be the most important influence of the Sangha in the political arena. The more lasting contribution is symbolized by the efforts of early 1964, which saw the beginnings of an ethos and a structure with some potential for overcoming the communalism and the regionalism that so badly divide South Vietnam.

In passing, it should be noted that while Vietnam may offer the most dramatic example of the political activism of the Sangha, it is by no means the only one. In Ceylon monks actively campaigned for the election of S.W.R.D. Bandaranaike and were influential in the defeat of his wife's race for reelection. She lost their support when she accepted backing from Ceylon's Communist Party. Today in Ceylon the great majority of politicians, regardless of their party, make speeches with monks at their side. Similarly, in Burma, U Nu had wide support in the Sangha, where the tradition of clerical involvement in the political sphere goes back to the 1920's when U Wisera became a nationalist martyr after he died in jail during a hunger strike to win the right to wear his robes while in prison. This kind of political involvement is met with diverse reactions in the countries involved. The militant wing of the United Buddhist Association in Vietnam lost some support from the moderate Buddhists. In Ceylon a limited poll of influential Buddhist laymen revealed that direct political activity was the least acceptable of all forms of Sangha participation in the sociopolitical realm. Yet, Buddhist monks can and do wield a powerful political influence. Sometimes it is used wisely. At other times the bhikkhu is merely exploited by political forces. On occasion the militant monks in Vietnam may have been used by the Viet Cong, and in Ceylon members of the Sangha are often utilized by politicians to win votes. In such circumstances the effectiveness of the monk as a social and political critic declines.

Within the traditions of Theravāda Buddhism the politically exploited bhikkhu is a reversal of the usual relationship between monk and layman. Traditionally the laymen played a role as the provider (*dayaka*) of the necessary material goods (e.g., food, robes) for the monk, thereby enabling the bhikkhu to maintain an aloofness from worldly concerns. When the monk becomes one of the chief vote-getters for the politician, he, in effect, becomes the *dayaka* for the layman. There are, undoubtedly, appropriate roles for monks to play in the political sphere, but the danger of sacrificing the perspective of the *religieux* is great. When that happens, the bhikkhu has nothing distinctive to offer, and the creative tension between the religious and the secular is lost.

We have examined only one model of Sangha participation in the sociopolitical realm. There are others, however. One that is becoming increasingly significant in countries such as Ceylon and Thailand is the activity of monks in the area of community development. In Thailand, where the Sangha has maintained its organization more intact

than in any other Southeast Asian country, the monk is
gradually moving into new and more socially involving
roles. This change has resulted primarily from innovations
in bhikkhu education (to be discussed in the following
chapter) and, more recently, the institution of monastic
training programs in social welfare and rural uplift. The
largest, most publicized, and most criticized of these has
been instituted by Phra Kitthiwuttho through the Abhidhamma Foundation of Wat Mahādhatu, which is the
center of the Mahānikāya, largest and oldest of the two
sects of Theravāda Buddhism in Thailand. Through this
program nearly one thousand monks have been brought to
Bangkok from the provinces to participate in training programs lasting from three to six months. Although these
programs have centered on the training of monks for the
propagation of Buddhism, they have also included courses
in the practical aspects of community development. The
majority of the monks graduating from this program, while
representing nearly all parts of Thailand, come mainly
from the Northeastern area. It is there that Thailand faces
the greatest political threat from Communist subversive
elements. Consequently, the program inevitably assumes
political overtones. The political significance of this effort
to engage monks in Thailand's more underdeveloped area
is also enhanced by two factors: the practice of having
graduates from the program work with government officials, and the large amount of financial support given to
Phra Kitthiwuttho's Abhidhamma Foundation by government leaders. Indeed, many of the monks in the program
met by the author conceived of their mission as twofold:
to propagate Buddhism and to combat Communism.

In order to guarantee a steady supply of well-trained,
committed bhikkhus willing to dedicate their lives to work

in poor, rural areas, Kitthiwuttho has founded a School for the Propagation of Buddhism in Chon Buri Province outside of Bangkok. Although opened only in 1968, it plans eventually to accommodate approximately fifteen hundred monks and novices from elementary through university levels. Kitthiwuttho, a handsome young man in his late thirties, has been extremely successful in raising money for the construction of school buildings. It is interesting to note that in a society where age and equanimity are venerated, especially in the Sangha, the leader of this community development enterprise is young, gregarious, and aggressive. Kitthiwuttho may well portend a different kind of life-style for at least a sector of the Thai monastic order, one that dedicates itself to social and political involvement rather than monastic withdrawal. He has been criticized for being overly "commercial" and "political," and other efforts within the Sangha have been held up as more exemplary of the ideals of Buddhism. In particular the ecclesiastical governor of Thonburi, the city on the opposite river side of Bangkok, has been lauded for his efforts to train monks as leaders in modern society. There can be little doubt that the informed engagement of the bhikkhu with Thailand's economic and social problems will prove to have significant consequences for the future of the Buddhist Sangha as well as the future of the Thai nation. In the long run, programs such as those of the Abhidhamma Foundation and other ecclesiastical agencies should help to bring about a new relevancy of Buddhism to Thailand and an increasingly valuable interplay between religion and society, the Sangha and the state.

In Ceylon, some of the most interesting projects involving monks in the social, political, and economic realms have been urged by Hema Henry Basnayake, a retired

Supreme Court chief justice now devoting most of his
time to rural uplift. Mr. Basnayake contends that monk
and layman must work hand in hand for the progress of
Ceylon. To bring about such cooperation he has urged the
formation of the Sangha Sabha (a council or assembly of
monks responsible for governing temple affairs) aimed
primarily at the improvement of the living conditions of
the peasant. The most important role to be played by the
monk, in Mr. Basnayake's approach, is that of a mediator
between the common man and the government. Because
of the position of trust and respect held by the temple
monks in local villages, he contends that they would be
the logical persons to represent the problems of the people
to the government. Mr. Basnayake has even suggested
that monks should function as justices of the peace in
order to expedite many government functions at the local
level.[29]

Of the schemes involving the participation of bhikkhus
in the community-development type of project, the most
ambitious undertaken by Mr. Basnayake is the Ceylon
Farmers' Association, an organization formed in 1966 with
a charter signed by four Maha Theras and five laymen.
Among the fifty-four stated objectives of the association is
included a variety of specific economic projects and also
the general aim "to provide for *the spiritual and material
welfare* of the people of Ceylon through the island through
the medium of the Sangha dedicated to the service of
mankind and the welfare of the country." [30] Supporters
of projects of this type contend that the monk has always
been a person concerned about the welfare of the people
and that only if monks take an active role in the secular
world will both the Sāsana and the nation progress.

Monastic involvement in secular affairs is not new to

Buddhism. Buddhist monks have always offered advice on social, political, and economic matters. There are, however, several aspects of the present situation that remain ambiguous. In particular the new roles being played by bhikkhus must be clarified; carefully delineated education and training must be made more adequate to these roles; and laymen and monk need to find new ways of working together in areas of community and national development. The place of the Buddhist monk is being severely challenged in this transitional period, especially in the eyes of the educated elite. Without careful attention to the future role of the monk, the contribution of Buddhism to the developing nations of Southeast Asia may be jeopardized

Buddhist Lay Organizations and Nationalism

The resurgence of Buddhism in Southeast Asia in the early part of this century was channeled in part through a number of Buddhist lay associations. Of special note in both Ceylon and Burma was the Y.M.B.A. (Young Men's Buddhist Association), obviously modeled after the Y.M.C.A. The political interests of these groups varied. In Burma the Y.M.B.A. was at the forefront of the nationalist movement in the 1920's. In Ceylon the Y.M.B.A. of Colombo gave rise to the All Ceylon Buddhist Congress, which had initially been formed as the All Ceylon Congress of Y.M.B.A.'s. Under the leadership of such nationally known figures as Dr. G. P. Malalasakera it rose to special prominence in the postindependence period. An umbrella organization for about three hundred different Buddhist groups, the congress has assumed the leadership role in promoting Buddhism on a national basis. Among its aims are to foster and protect the interests and privileges of Buddhists, to promote cooperation among Buddhist groups, to represent Buddhists in public matters affecting their interests, and to undertake Buddhist charitable activities. Whereas it engages in a wide variety of social services ranging from orphanages to helping to care for Buddhist antiquities, one of the principal ways in which it fulfills those aims associated with representing Buddhist interests is to act as a political pressure group.

The congress was the principal exponent of the Poya[31] day holiday (rather than Sunday) and has encouraged the government to enforce the closure of bars, meat stalls, cinemas, and social clubs on those days. Also the congress has called upon the government to enact and enforce prohibition laws and has urged the appointment of a press council to oversee a responsible press. And it has suggested that the government incorporate into the national constitution a bill of rights that would redress the grievances of Buddhists who have suffered discrimination in public services or employment in corporations and private businesses.

The most significant undertaking of the congress was the appointment of a Buddhist Committee of Inquiry in April, 1954, with the task of inquiring into "the present state of Buddhism in Ceylon and to report on the conditions necessary to improve and strengthen the position of Buddhism and the means whereby these conditions may be fulfilled." [32] The result of the committee's study was a scathing denunciation of the treatment Buddhists had received under European Christian colonial rulers:

> In its travels in various parts of the island, the Committee had ample opportunities to observe at first hand the harassment and obstruction placed in the way of Buddhists in all spheres of life, education, social services, hospitals and so on. The time has em-

phatically arrived when the Buddhists need to be
strong, united and steadfast for the struggle.[33]

The report of the committee was published in 1956 and
was probably instrumental in the election of S.W.R.D.
Bandaranaike, who pledged himself and his party to support its recommendations. The report captured the imagination of a large section of the Buddhist public and
coincided with the Buddha Jayanti celebration to fan the
flames of Buddhist nationalism to a white-hot heat.

The recommendations of the report covered a wide area.
A particular thrust was an attempt to strengthen the
Sangha through the creation of an overarching Sangha
organization, a sequence of ecclesiastical courts, and a solution to the problem of the ownership of temple lands.
Other recommendations dealt with social conditions. The
report lamented the moral tone of the country and recommended a revolutionary displacement of "Western materialistic social and individual values" and the establishment of "genuine values founded on the Buddha
Dhamma." [34] These values would be encouraged by the
prohibition of intoxicants, banning of horse racing, wearing
national dress, encouraging plain living and obedience to
sīla, i.e., the precepts of lay Buddhism.[35] In one sense the
report was highly traditionalistic and moralistic. Yet, as
G. C. Mendis points out, it was revolutionary in that it
ignored the traditional Buddhist assumptions of kamma
and saṁsāra and the ideal of withdrawal from the world.[36]
It offered a program of positive action that would restore
Ceylon to her true heritage based on the values of Buddhism.

A major question about the program of the All Ceylon
Buddhist Congress is its overbearing moralistic preoccupation. The annual reports of the congress reiterate the old

problems of prohibition, press regulation, and so on. When the author was in Ceylon in 1967 a major anxiety of the congress was the corrupting influence of the miniskirt. The role of the congress would be enhanced if it directed more of its energies to the interrelationship of Buddhism and some of the major social and economic problems Ceylon faces rather than repeatedly warning the youth about the dangers of arrack, horse racing, and miniskirts. The congress proved its power as a pressure group in urging the passage of a bill to secure the Poya day holiday. It remains to be seen whether it can offer distinctive leadership in pursuing solutions to the more pressing issues of national concern.

In East Asia the Buddhist lay organization with the most widely publicized political potential is Soka Gakkai (Value-Creating Society), the layman's association of the Nichiren Sho Shu in Japan.[37] Although Nichiren Sho Shu traces its history back to the time of Nichiren himself (thirteenth century) and considers itself to represent the true form of Nichiren's teachings, the Soka Gakkai is of much later origin. It was founded in 1937 by a retired schoolteacher, Makiguchi Tsunesaburo, and under its subsequent leaders, Toda Josei (1951–1958) and Daisaku Ikeda (1960–   ), has become one of the most powerful popular movements in the history of Japan. James A. Dator analyzes the Soka Gakkai as a mass movement produced by the frustrations and anxieties accompanying the disintegration of a once compact social structure.[38] In particular, he sees it fulfilling the relative deprivation gap characterizing certain sectors of Japanese society whose gains have not kept pace with the contemporary revolution in rising social and economic standards. Soka Gakkai offers progress to an ideal state in which personal alienation is overcome, presenting a personal/group solution to the cultural value crisis following World War II. Felix Moos, in more descriptive terms, says that Soka Gakkai meetings, as well as the closely knit Soka Gakkai organization, "impart to the participant a deep sense of belonging —to a spiritual elite of the one and only faith—and offer, particularly in Japan's ever-growing urban areas, an escape from the loneliness and isolation of mass society." [39] Whatever the cause for its success—the psychological fulfillment it offers, the evangelistic zeal of its members, or its militarylike organization—Soka Gakkai claims a membership of over six and one half million households and is the largest voluntary organization in Japan, embracing more than 10 percent of the total population. [40]

Soka Gakkai has evolved both a political philosophy and a political party. The party, known as the Komeito or Clean Government Party, has since 1962 been the third largest party in the Upper House of the Japanese Diet and followed an impressive record in the 1968 summer elections with additional gains in the winter of 1969. On the basis of the poor showing of the Socialist Party in the 1968 and 1969 elections, some Soka Gakkai officials are predicting that in the next national election the Komeito Party will be second to the ruling Liberal Democrats, and that in the following election they will come out on top. Such a prediction was made to the author in an interview held at the Tokyo headquarters of Soka Gakkai. It was conducted with great assurance and conviction, bolstered by an impressive cinemascope film of the Soka Gakkai 1966 summer cultural festival held in the Tokyo Olympic stadium, in which thousands of participants acted and danced out the theme of building eternal peace through Soka Gakkai.

The political philosophy expounded by the Soka Gakkai

might also be labeled as Buddhist socialism, a term used in conjunction with both U Nu and S.W.R.D. Bandaranaike. Manipulating the well-known epithet applied to Buddhism as the religion of the Middle Way, Soka Gakkai advocates a middle-of-the-road government. It means a middle way between capitalism and communism, a way that "rests on the basis of the dignity of life and respect for humanity; . . . aims at the construction of a new society based upon harmony and mutual trust; . . . is designed to realize true democracy; . . . aims at realizing true public welfare;" and "intends to realize 'a warless world,' that is to ensure that eternal peace which mankind has long embraced as an ideal." [41] Coupled with these idealistic generalizations are some politically savvy, concrete proposals. For example, since 1966 and 1967 the Komeito Party has consistently advocated that the Japan-U.S. Security Treaty be *gradually* dissolved. This position reflected both the prevailing opinion of the Japanese public and a more realistic political position than either the Liberal Democrats or the Socialists had yet adopted. It may well be that the Soka Gakkai arrived at this formulation as a consequence of information received from their network of Public Counseling Centers located all over Japan, surely one of the most astute political mechanisms devised by any political party.

The future of Soka Gakkai is uncertain. Its arm-twisting methods have created a strong negative reaction among many Japanese. In particular, the leaders of the more traditional Buddhist sects criticize them for using the trappings of religion to justify the building of a political force. It must be said in its defense, however, that its founder, Nichiren, was a highly nationalistic religious leader who saw himself as the prophet of the true Buddhism and Japan as the country from which it would be propagated.

Although the methods of Soka Gakkai are obviously not those of the thirteenth century, their aggressive zeal is partly in keeping with the founder of the Buddhist sect with which Soka Gakkai claims affiliation.

Soka Gakkai's partnership with Nichiren Sho Shu is extremely important to its success. This relationship gives it an affiliation with a uniquely Japanese form of Buddhism with a six-hundred-year-old tradition. As a result, Soka Gakkai has acquired an aura of authenticity that some of the so-called new religions in Japan lack, as well as a justification for its strong nationalistic bias and militant evangelistic methods. Of even greater consequence, however, is the symbolic value derived from the head temple of Taisekiji at Oishi-ga-hara (Field of Great Stones) near Mt. Fuji where the Dai-Gohonzon of Nichiren is reputed to be enshrined. Soka Gakkai claims this mandala represents the quintessence of Nichiren's mission and is their chief object of worship along with the prophet himself and the Lotus Sutra. Mt. Fuji, of course, is the most holy of all the sacred mountains in Japan and functions as the mythological axis around which the nation's existence revolves. The holy grounds near Mt. Fuji have been effectively appropriated by Soka Gakkai and now house the Dai-Kodo (Grand Lecture Hall), the tomb of Josei Toda, and construction has begun on a multi-million-dollar Sho-Hondo (Grand Main Temple) to be completed by 1972.

The days of the absolute monarchs on whose favor the Buddhist Sangha relied and on whose support the monarchs, in turn, depended for some semblance of national unity and coherence are long past. Yet, the ideas and the cultural ideals of Buddhism live on, in many cases with an enhanced value as the means by which developing

Asian nations might weather the storms of change and crisis. We have seen that some Asian leaders have been extraordinarily sensitive to the role that Buddhism can play as the basis of a national ideology to create the esprit necessary for progress and development. The Sangha, as well, is beginning to move in the direction of more involvement in the sociopolitical realm and to look forward to an education that will prepare bhikkhus with practical as well as religious skills. And, finally, we have noted a new phenomenon, the banding together of laymen whose self-consciousness as Buddhists was reoriented through the impact of Western (especially Christian) organizational patterns. Whether or not these and other responses will be an adequate means by which Buddhism might take an active part in the process of nation-building is not at all clear. Even apparent failures such as U Nu are difficult to evaluate. It is apparent, however, that the most viable and enduring nations in Southeast Asia will be those where Buddhism as a life orientation and as an institution makes the necessary adaptations to participate critically and creatively in the ongoing processes of change.

III

BUDDHISM
AND "CULTURAL REVOLUTION"

The term "cultural revolution" evokes images of Red Guards running riot in Shanghai, political purges in Peking, and newspaper posters describing the ouster of reactionary elements in Canton. Yet, the rubric should not be confined to its Maoist connotations, for to a profound degree much of Asia is undergoing a cultural revolution of its own. For example, in Japan the tea ceremony is being replaced by Western-style coffee shops serving spaghetti and waffles, in Thailand the king plays a jazz cornet, and Coca-Cola rivals Colgate toothpaste as the most pervasive bearer of Western civilization all over Asia! Some countries are resisting this kind of Westernization: Prince Sihanouk felt compelled to rebuff Western influence in order to remain neutral; many Ceylonese think Western values are corrupting; and in Burma, in what must epitomize the rejection of American influence, even the support of the Advanced Institute of Buddhistic Studies by the Ford Foundation has been eliminated.

One aspect of the Asian cultural revolution is the response Buddhism is making to modernization under the impact of the West. Typologically this response has taken the form of accommodation, rejection, or an interaction in which Buddhism addresses itself to different kinds of problems, recasts its institutional structures, or renovates its modes of thought. This interaction has produced some interesting developments, especially in the areas of Buddhist social ethics, Buddhist education, Buddhism and scientific thought, and a variety of expressions of Buddhism as a world religion. We shall look briefly at each of these developments.

BUDDHIST SOCIAL ETHICS[1]

"The development of a Buddhist social ethic, and the organizational means to apply it to contemporary problems, are the pressing requirements of our times." [2] "Buddhism must have a new birth. . . . It would be a Social Religion. . . . It would pursue not a will-o'-the-wisp Nirvāna . . . but a Nirvāna attained here and now by a life of self-forgetful activity." [3] The first of these two quotations is by an American political scientist who has written extensively on the problem of religion and politics in Asia. The second is from *The Revolt in the Temple,* a controversial book by a Ceylonese critically describing the national religious situation as it had developed up to the time of the Buddha Jayanti celebration in 1956. Both agree that Buddhism in Ceylon must become more socially relevant, especially through a reformation of the Sangha. They are joined in this opinion by many others who optimistically see the beginnings of such a development taking place. However, classical Theravāda Buddhism offers a number of problems to the articulation of a social ethic. They include: a search for an ultimate goal

(Nibbāna) demanding absolute detachment and an equanimity transcending ethical distinctions; a suspicion of the phenomenal world as a sphere of sensory attachment and bondage to illusory conceptions (e.g., the notion of a Self, *atta*); a predominantly asocially conceived monastic institution (Sangha) relatively isolated from the laity; and a social philosophy based on the thesis that the betterment of society comes about only through the betterment of individuals. Some questions resulting from this stance are: Can the ultimate goal become more intrinsically a part of relative ethical behavior? Is it possible to couple a positive ethic with a negative view of the world? In what way can the Sangha develop a *modus vivendi* of greater social responsiveness? and, How can problems basically social in nature be handled by a religion essentially individualistic in character? In fairness to Theravāda Buddhism it must be said that questions such as these are, to a certain extent, more logical or theoretical in nature than actual. As K. N. Jayatilleke points out in criticism of Arnold Toynbee's *An Historian's Approach to Religion,* it is not a fair reading of the Pāli texts to say that Nibbāna is intrinsically unattainable.[4] Furthermore, from a sociological perspective, the distinction between a relative world conditioned by *kamma* and *saṁsāra* and an unconditioned, absolute realm of Nibbāna is not really so neatly clear-cut. Despite this qualifier, any discussion of contemporary efforts to formulate a Buddhist social ethic must take into account some of these problems and resultant questions.

Regarding the conception of Nibbāna, the opening quotation from *The Revolt in the Temple* represents one of the most consistent themes in the recasting of the ideal of a radical, otherworldly salvation. One might describe it as a kind of Buddhist Social Gospel–Kingdom of God on earth notion. This transformation of Nibbāna into an immanent, if not an imminent, ideal is expressed in both individual and collective dimensions. Individually, Nibbāna is made a more realizable goal through the practice of meditation. We have seen how important meditation was for U Nu. In fact, in some ways it was the cornerstone of his religiously conceived, socialistic state. If individuals would practice meditation, they would experience a higher degree of self-control and selflessness and a greater commitment to the good of others rather than to their own self-interest. Meditation on the part of individuals, therefore, would result in a better nation. This emphasis on meditation by laymen is a unique phenomenon in the history of Buddhism. Whereas the goal of Nibbāna was not necessarily the exclusive preserve of the monk-meditator, the layman rarely practiced the meditative disciplines. Largely due to developments in Burma in recent years, lay meditation centers are now found in Colombo, Rangoon, Bangkok, and elsewhere in Southeast Asia. By emphasizing the positive results of meditation for the lives of peoples engaging in secular vocations, Buddhism is attempting to give its ultimate goal more social relevance. Westerners for whom social ethics tend to be more structural than psychophysical may scoff that such efforts are unrealistic and cannot correct problems basically societal in nature. No doubt this kind of criticism is valid; however, without arguing the point, the attempts of the West to cope with its social problems cannot be said to have met with resounding success!

Nibbāna as an attainable ideal operates in a kind of realized-eschatological way. Buddhists in both Burma and Ceylon have synthesized socialism and Buddhism into an ideal that glorifies spiritual ends but acknowledges the importance of material necessities. This view holds that working only for material gain such as private wealth or personal property will lead to attachment (hence, capitalism is rejected), but that spiritual aims can be realized only when physical needs are assuaged. Supporting this position, they cite the incident in the Buddha's own enlightenment quest when he gave up the practice of extreme austerities and adopted a Middle Way between extravagance and self-denial. In a similar fashion, Buddhists should strive for a "cooperative commonwealth," which will be a synthesis of Nibbāna-ideals with socialistic economic methods.

Nibbāna as an ideal social order in which the ultimate aim of each person can be realized combines both collective and individual elements. The individual aspect relates not only to the traditional Buddhist atomistic notion of salvation but to a social ideal as well. The ideal Buddhist society would be both socialistic *and* democratic. Just as the Sangha of old was ordered so that individuals governed themselves by common consent, the ideal Buddhist social order should be organized around egalitarian methods. Not only will democratic political methods be more just and humane; they will also offer greater individual freedom for the realization of ultimate goals. With a Mahāyānistic philosophical slant, Daisaku Ikeda describes Buddhism as the basis of democracy as follows: "Buddhism is not a religion in which each member of society establishes his own independence and becomes the ruler of his own environment. In Buddhism, the Buddha and the ordinary man are not juxtaposed, but are one and the same." [5] The Soka Gakkai vision of the ideal society more easily combines the transcendent ideal

with worldly realities. In the Theravāda scheme, the ideal
society would be one that would allow for higher individual self-realization.

In a quest for a viable social ethic, other typical Buddhist notions are being emphasized, applied to different
contexts, or transformed. The past deterministic aspect of
kamma is being diverted, and the possibility of conditioning future situations is being accentuated. The *bodhisatta* ideal of the compassionate wisdom-being, a major
theme in Mahāyāna Buddhism but largely ignored in
classical Theravāda Buddhism, is being refurbished. It is
related to the life of the Buddha, the tolerant, compassionate, understanding teacher, and to stories of the
previous lives of the Buddha (the Jātaka) which often
stress the ideal of self-giving. Buddhist texts dealing with
social ethics, such as the Mangala, Mettā, and Sigāla Suttas, are being reprinted in separate editions, discussed in lay
Buddhist associations and preached about in Sabbath Day
services. The four ideals or states of mind associated with
meditation, known as the Divine Abodes (*brahma vihāra*)
or Illimitables (*appamaññā*), are being given a social
significance, especially *mettā* ("love") and *karuṇa* ("compassion"), the first two of these ideal states.

Colonel Pin Mutugan, the highest-ranking official in the
Department of Religion of the Ministry of Education in
Thailand, describes *mettā-karuṇā* together as sacrificial
and self-giving love, the kind of love a parent has toward
his child in contrast to a selfish love whose concern for
others is only in terms of one's own self-aggrandizement.[6]
The highest type of love, he affirms, is infused with
uppekkhā (equanimity, the fourth of the Four Illimitables). Love coupled with *uppekkhā* is a love that grows
more neutral the greater the attachment becomes. As Col-

onel Pin aphoristically states: "He who is conquered by love loses control of himself. He who conquers love is master of himself." [7] Only when men are able to conquer love as a selfish attachment does it become useful and beneficial. A stable family can be built only on a self-giving, altruistic love. Love, says Pin, is like a river. When one bathes near the bank it is enjoyable, cooling, and comforting. But if a person goes into deep water over his head, the water may get the best of him.[8] In like manner, the highest and most salutary love must be instilled with the caution of *upekkhā*.

Contemporary popular expositions on the theme of love generally are given a very practical thrust. The intent seems to be to teach people how to lead a good life rather than to reflect on the nature of existence as impermanent and causally conditioned. Thus, Bhikkhu Paññānanda, one of Thailand's most famous monks, defines *mettā-karuṇā* as a love that is self-sacrificing and self-forgetting, a love that "helps one's neighbor." He admonishes people who feel sorry for the less fortunate person, such as a leper, but do nothing to help him. It is not enough to have *mettā* toward those who need help. One must have the compassion (*karuṇā*) to help them out of their misery in order to appreciate the third level of the Illimitables, known as *mudita* (sympathetic joy). "Those who are strong must help the weak; those who are rich must help the poor; those who are clever must help the foolish." [9] According to Bhikkhu Paññānanda, love is sacrifice. Real love is the cause of happiness and peace. It is the love of bright, sensitive, intelligent people. Real love does not blind a person. On the contrary, it is illuminating. Possessing love composed of the Four Illimitables, *mettā*, *karuṇā*, *mudita*, and *upekkhā*, does not mean simply that one is reborn into a better existence. It means that one will have good benefits in this life as well. To the degree that one has *mettā* in depth and breadth, to that degree one will have happiness as well.[10]

To the extent that the major emphasis of much contemporary discussion of personal and social ethics focuses on effective ways to live in the world, Theravāda Buddhism reflects an adaption to new environmental conditions. It should not be thought, however, that a concern for structuring viable social relationships is new to Buddhism. As we have consistently maintained, it is a misunderstanding of traditional Theravāda Buddhism to label it as simply world-denying. It would appear that in many cases a serious attempt is being made to synthesize some of the traditional concepts of Buddhism with insights derived from the modern context in such a way that hitherto neglected aspects of Buddhist thought come to take their rightful place. The method by which this is done may often sound old-fashioned or even naïve to the sophisticated Westerner; however, to appreciate properly the efforts to devise a relevant social ethic the Westerner must also be able to understand the customs, life-style, and literary tradition of the Asian. In doing so, he might be less quick to dismiss these efforts as irrelevant and ineffective.

Perhaps the best way to summarize some of the most important themes in the contemporary quest for an ethical posture that would provide both practical guidance and an ideal aim is to let a Ceylonese Buddhist leader speak for himself:

Buddhism aims at creating a society where the ruinous struggle for power is renounced; where calm and peace prevail away from conquest and defeat; where the persecution of the innocent is vehemently denounced; where one who conquers oneself is more respected than those who conquest millions by military and economic warfare; where hatred is conquered by kindness, and evil by goodness; where enmity, jealousy, ill-will and greed do not infect men's minds; where compassion is the driving force of action; where all, including the least of living things, are treated with fairness, consideration and love; where life in peace and harmony, in a world of material contentment, is directed towards the highest and noblest aim, the realization of Ultimate Truth, Nirvāna.[11]

BUDDHIST EDUCATION[12]

Historically one of the most important functions performed by the Sangha was education, for until the advent of European colonial powers and Christian missionaries nearly all education took place within the precincts of the temple grounds. Even with the establishment of secular educational institutions monks played an important role as teachers of Buddhist doctrine, history, and ethics. Gradually, however, their importance as educators waned, and in most instances the monks not only lost their hold over educational matters but they themselves fell far behind the pace of secular education. The bhikkhus' education was confined largely to religious topics and they knew little of the content of modern academic disciplines. This educational gap is one of the reasons that the Sangha, especially in urban areas, lost much of the respect it once had among the elites of Asian society.

With the advent of movements for independence in such countries as Ceylon and Burma, attention was

turned to efforts to rectify the sad plight of the Sangha
vis à vis education. In Ceylon, for example, education
was one of the most important areas in which the revival
of Buddhism took shape, due in part to the direct influence of Colonel Henry Steel Olcott, but more generally
because the Buddhists were convinced that the English-
language Christian schools' monopoly on education had
to be broken if Buddhism was to survive. In 1880, for
instance, there were fewer than 100 Buddhist schools
compared with nearly 900 Christian schools.[13] Under
Olcott's leadership and with the assistance of other prominent theosophists, over 200 Buddhist schools and three
colleges were established of which the foremost was
Ananda College in Colombo, founded in 1886.

Concerned Buddhist laymen view the rise of Buddhist
educational institutions with pride. Sentiments such as
the following are typical:

> In the race against Christian institutions, schools like
> Ananda left the best and oldest mission schools far
> behind. . . . Today in the highest echelons of the
> public service, medicine, science, law, engineering,
> education, government and politics, are the brilliant
> products of Ananda and its sister institutions. The
> best service rendered the country and the Sinhala
> race is that of training Buddhist children in a na-
> tional atmosphere, to revere their religion, customs
> and culture.[14]

Because of this pride in a specifically Buddhist-oriented
education, many laymen have registered a strong negative
opinion regarding the nationalization of schools in 1964.
They contend that the take-over, rather than bolstering
the cause of Buddhism, has hindered it. In particular, it

is felt that such well-known colleges as Ananda, Mahinda, and Dharmaraja are no longer centers of Buddhist learning and culture, that a religious atmosphere had been replaced by a secular one, and that there is an increasingly "rapid degeneration and moral decay of the rising generation of our children." [15]

A similar negative response has been evoked regarding the "secularization" of the monks' higher education. Those who feel that the bhikkhus' training should be confined strictly to religious subjects object to monks being enrolled as regular students at the state universities. They are also unhappy with the decision made by S.W.R.D. Bandaranaike to elevate the monastic Pirivenas of Vidyodaya and Vidyalankara in Colombo to university status, admitting lay students as well as bhikkhus. The following is a common reaction:

The Buddhist public are naturally embarrassed and dismayed to find Bhikkhus in vehicles, with brief cases tucked under their arms, looking quite brisk and business-like, meticulously handling money, haunting shops, cinemas and public places, with all the materialistic fervor of dedicated worldlings. Teaching in Pirivenas and other places to enthusiastic groups of students, including diverse females is another alarming factor . . . which will eventually lead to the complete corruption and dissolution of the Sangha.[16]

In spite of a critical response on the part of the more traditional and conservative segments of the Buddhist community in Ceylon, it is important that these changes have taken place. As a consequence, bhikkhus who desire higher education are being trained not only in some of the rudiments of Buddhist doctrine and methods of chanting the Buddhist Suttas (scriptures) but in a wide variety of secular subjects. If the Sangha is to progress and engage the contemporary world with some degree of understanding and relevance, such changes in the monks' education are essential. Although the intermeshing of monastic and lay education at the university level may be disputed from a number of perspectives, especially the quality of the education at the former Pirivenas in Colombo, the need to upgrade them was apparent.

The revival of Buddhist education in Ceylon took place not only through the development of Buddhist schools. Two important lay organizations contributing to this field were the Y.M.B.A. of Colombo and the Maha Bodhi Society. The latter was founded by the Anagarika Dharmapala in 1891 and continues its educational function through public lectures at its center in Colombo, the publication of an English-language journal, *The Mahabodhi,* and the only Sinhalese Buddhist weekly publication, the *Sinhala Bauddha.* The Y.M.B.A. conducts Dhamma (doctrine, teachings) schools and Dhamma examinations at Y.M.B.A. centers and temples around the country. They are aimed at providing "the youth of the land with the same standard of religious instruction and Buddhist education as was imparted by the Maha Sangha in the temple schools in times before foreigners destroyed that great national institution." [17]

In the light of both certain aspects of the Buddhist educational revival (e.g., the traditional nature of the Y.M.B.A. Dhamma examinations) and the negative reactions other changes have produced (e.g., monks attending secular universities), one wonders whether contemporary Buddhist education in Ceylon will be able to speak with relevance to the needs of a society in transition. If the quotation above reflects a typical attitude toward the revival of Buddhist education, its ability to cope with change will, at best, be seriously hampered.

In Burma and Thailand, Buddhist education on the school level suffered badly in the competition with both secular state and private Christian schools. One of U Nu's campaign pledges in the election of 1961 was to revive Buddhist education and the role of the Sangha in it. In Thailand some of the most interesting developments have been taking place on the level of monastic institutions of higher education. For over a decade the two Buddhist universities, Mahāmakut and Mahāchulalongkorn, have been making strides toward modernizing their educational programs. Of these two institutions, Mahāchulalongkorn, the university of the largest Theravāda sect in Thailand, appears to have taken the lead in the effort to broaden its curriculum beyond the traditional courses in Pāli, Thai, and Buddhist doctrine and practice. Within the Faculty of Humanities and Social Welfare are offered courses in sociology, hygiene, economics, government, and law, as well as studies in art, archaeology, geography, and history. Such a broadening of the curriculum and expansion of the teaching staff to include teachers from government universities and various professional services represent an effort to respond to the felt need to equip Buddhist monks with a scope of knowledge more relevant to the contemporary world. As Phra Mahā Prayuddha, the assistant secretary general of the university, points out, in the past Buddhist monks and laymen had an intimate rapport with each other because the milieus in which they lived were much the same. Today, however, the widening gap between the life of the layman (especially in urban areas) and that of the bhikkhu demands that monks receive a more broadly designed training. "It is not," asserts Phra

Mahā Prayuddha, "that we are trying to secularize the Buddhist monk. Rather we are attempting to restore him to his traditional place as religious leader and guide of the people." As he stated in a sermon on the social responsibilities of the monk, "Besides their own peculiar duties toward the goal of self-enlightenment, monks are bound with many social obligations to serve their community and to render reasonable service for the benefit of the layman's society." For this service they must be properly educated and trained. Leaders of the two Buddhist universities in Thailand such as Phra Mahā Prayuddha are not interested in *accommodating* Buddhism to the demands of a rapidly changing world, but they are decidedly concerned about its relevance to such a world. They are convinced that the Sangha can survive in the modern age only if it studies the secular disciplines. Otherwise they feel that Buddhism will become an irrelevant part of Thailand's heritage rather than involved in a living present.[18]

To help fulfill its aims Mahāchulalongkorn University supports a number of programs other than its university faculties. For example, the Buddhist Sunday School Movement, begun in 1958 by an American-educated university administrator, represents an attempt to improve the understanding of Buddhism among laymen. The university also began a program in 1966 to encourage its graduates to take teaching positions in rural areas. Training covers not only subjects dealing specifically with Buddhism but also public health, community development, vocational promotion, village leadership development, public relations, and applied psychology. Instruction not only takes place at the university but includes field work in one of the provinces in Northeastern Thailand, and plans are now in progress to establish coordinate training programs in provincial monasteries in other parts of Thailand.

A number of problems remain to be solved. A major one is the adoption of techniques and institutional forms from the West without any basic change of content or insight into the nature of creative educational reform. Frequently a program will look innovative on paper but be sadly lacking in execution. L. G. Hewage, professor of education at Vidyodaya Buddhist University in Colombo, has summarized some of the most urgent questions of Buddhist higher education as follows: (1) What should be the role of Buddhist studies in secular universities? (2) How can Buddhist studies be made more effective in universities? (3) How can Buddhist studies be popularized as an integral part of a general education course, as well as a specialized field of study? (4) What plan of action is sensible and practicable in promoting an all-pervading influence among university staff and students as a result of the study of Buddhism? (5) What aspects or areas of Buddha Dhamma and Buddhist culture are appropriate to be included in the university curriculum? (6) What university reforms should be undertaken to enrich the experiences of young people who study everything else but Buddhism? (7) What role should Buddhist monks play in Buddhist higher education? (8) What secular subjects should be included in the education of monks and lay teachers of Buddhism? (9) Should plans be made with the World Fellowship of Buddhists for a World Institute of Buddhist Education? [19] These kinds of questions offer some insight into the shape of Buddhist educational reform. Although parochial to a certain degree, they also point to new directions that may be taken in the revival of Buddhism through education.

BUDDHISM AND SCIENTIFIC THOUGHT[20]

Buddhism has adopted an ambivalent attitude toward modern science. Negatively it sees in the scientific attitude an unwillingness to admit the validity of spiritual truth and a threat not only to Buddhism but to other religions as well. Hence, it is not uncommon in Asia today to find Buddhists calling for a united front on the part of all religions against a scientism critical of religious values and truths. Positively, however, many Buddhists would claim that Buddhism is the most scientific of all religions and has nothing to fear from science. As U Chan Htoon, former justice of the Supreme Court of Burma, puts it: "In the case of Buddhism . . . all the modern scientific concepts have been present from the beginning. There is no principle of science, from biological evolution to the General Theory of Relativity, that runs counter to any teaching of Gotama Buddha." [21] "There cannot be any achievement of science, no matter how revolutionary, that will ever contradict the teachings of Buddhism." [22] Claims almost as grandiose are made by the Thai medical doctor Luang Suriyabongs in his book *Buddhism in the Light of Modern Scientific Ideas.* Some Western scholars even lend support to this position. Professor von Glasenapp, the noted German Indologist, sees intellectual affinities between modern philosophic and scientific ideas and the following notions in Buddhism: the principle of universal order (*dhamma*); a positivistic denial of eternal substances; the contention that soul or self is an artificial abstraction; the recognition of a plurality of worlds; and the affirmation of the essential similarity between man and animal.[23]

There are at least three principal ways in which the assertion of the scientific nature of Buddhism is presented: Buddhism is more scientific than other religions, especially theism (viz., Christianity); there is a general agreement between the approach or method of Buddhism and science; and, science proves or validates particular Buddhist teachings such as the doctrines of rebirth (*saṁsāra*) and impermanence (*anicca*). The Buddhist contention of a greater scientific validity than Christianity stems not only from the conflicts that have arisen between the Biblical world view and modern scientific hypotheses, but from the historical relationship between Christianity and Buddhism in Asia. During the period of colonial rule, Buddhism was looked upon by many, especially Christian missionaries, as an inferior, heathen religion of a backward people. The revival of Buddhism coincident with the independence movement created a new Buddhist apologetic gauged in part to justify Buddhism vis à vis Christianity. A portion of that apologetic, which runs strong even today in countries such as Ceylon and Burma, is to discredit Christianity as unscientific and to affirm the scientific nature of Buddhism not in terms of science, per se, but in contrast to theistic religions. Thus, Buddhist apologists (often writing in English!) pride themselves in being able to reject the theistic notions of an absolute deity, an immortal soul, and the question of first cause or prime mover, all theological dilemmas in the light of scientific discoveries. The absence of these ideas in Buddhism provokes the claim that Buddhism, consequently, is scientific and Christianity is unscientific: "Buddhism is the only religion which by itself and not without taking recourse to any God-entity can give a complete explanation . . . of all the Teachings of the Buddha because they

are based upon Universal laws." [24] Discrediting theistic
religions on the grounds that they are unscientific, some
apologists postulate that Buddhism, because of its scientific nature, is the most acceptable religion for the modern
world.

The approach or method of both science and Buddhism
is said to be inductive or experimental. There is no re-
liance on an outside authority nor any deduction from
hypothesis or assumption. Proof comes only through testing. On the theoretical side, Buddhism claims to be
empirical since it deals only with phenomena that can
be perceived (either by the senses or extrasensorily). The
truth of Buddhism is not to be inferred, but *seen*. On the
practical side, the discipline of meditation becomes the
experimental laboratory. Meditation is the means of testing the validity of the Buddha's claims. (It is said, for
example, that when U Nu was making speeches on Buddhism in the United States in 1956 he invited anyone who
wanted to test the truth of Buddhism to come to Burma
at his government's expense to practice meditation.) Although similarities are found between the approach to
truth in science and in Buddhism, the truth discovered
is acknowledged to be different: "The Buddha did not
teach science. He taught the Dhamma (Truth). The
Buddha-Truth is absolute. It cannot be proved by science
nor by any other method, except by intuitive insight, each
for himself." [25] At this point Buddhism parts company
with the physical or "hard" sciences but takes pleasure in
pointing out that the "mentalistic sciences" such as psychology have much in common with Buddhist teachings.

Several Buddhist teachings are singled out as being
either proved by science or scientific in character. They include, in particular, the doctrines of no-self (*anatta*), uni-

versal impermanence (*anicca*), moral causation (*kamma*), and rebirth (*saṁsāra*). Buddhist apologists observe that many forms of Western psychology either reject the concept of a Self or radically qualify it. Gordon W. Allport, for example, criticizes the use of the concept on the grounds that "the ego may be regarded as a *deus ex machina*" which psychologists invoke to give some coherence to the human personality after positivistic analysis has torn it into pieces.[26] Allport suggests that separate personality aspects or characteristics be used rather than the concept of a unifying ego or self. Although Allport's categories are radically different from Buddhism's, this suggestion is not unlike the view of the Buddhist who contends that the concept of a Self is an unfounded inference. In the Buddhist view there is no Ego or Self, but only a collection of aggregates or characteristics (i.e., body, sensations, perceptions, intentions, consciousness) that together form a human being. The Buddhist objection to the concept of Self, however, is not made primarily on scientific but on moral grounds. For Allport, the ego concept may have unfortunate consequences for psychotherapy; for the Buddhist, it is the Self or the Ego which is at the root of human acquisitiveness. If the Ego can be overcome, then the evils of hatred, delusion, and greed will also be transcended.

A second teaching that Buddhists find confirmed in science is the idea of impermanence or universal flux (*anicca*). In the Buddhist's view, nothing in the world is permanent, but all is in a constant process of change. Material and mental entities are composed of minute interrelated particles in a continual process of dying and being reborn. Buddhist apologists believe that this doctrine is, in general, confirmed by the dynamic physics of the

Einstein age, that matter is now understood in terms of energy, fields of force, and vibrations.[27] Mahāyāna Buddhists, such as Daisaku Ikeda, look upon the field theory of modern physics as confirmation of the Buddhist teaching of the inseparability of body and mind or matter and space. He quotes Einstein on the theory of the relationship of matter, energy, and field as follows:

> From the relativity theory we know that matter represents vast stores of energy and that energy represents matter. We cannot, in this way, distinguish qualitatively between matter and field, since the distinction between matter and energy is not a qualitative one. . . . We cannot imagine a definite surface separating distinctly field and matter.[28]

Ikeda himself concludes, "It is an astonishing fact that this idea of Einstein approaches closely the Buddhist idea of Ku or Shiki-shin Funi (inseparability of body and mind)," and in a footnote observes that field theory physics explains the essence of Buddhism in scientific terms— "though not perfectly." [29] Buddhists may use science, as Ikeda does in this instance, to explain Buddhism in a terminology acceptable to the modern mind or to prove Buddhist teachings. Or, as is often the case, they may conclude that Buddhism is actually superior to science, since a recent scientific discovery was anticipated by the Buddha twenty-five hundred years earlier!

Perhaps the Buddhist teachings receiving the greatest attention are rebirth (saṁsāra) and moral causation (kamma), two doctrines that are essentially related to each other. Kamma, in brief, is the theory that every action reaps a deserved result, that an evil action bears evil consequences, and a good action bears good consequences. As a general theory, there is agreement with the Western understanding of causality, namely, that a cause is an event or state preceding another event or state in time without which the latter would not occur.[30] Causation in the Buddhist view in general is that all events are interdependently related since they are part of a universe constantly involved in interactive change; however, it is also specific, especially in relationship to human action. The particular concern of Buddhism is to prove from the theory of general causation that human actions are causally related in a specific manner as, for example, in the formula of Dependent Origination (*paṭicca-samuppāda*) and that if the causal sequence is understood, it then becomes possible to transcend the bondage to causally conditioned behavior. In one sense, the Buddhist notion of *kamma* has something in common with positivistic behaviorism, but in another, it is radically different. There is the confidence that knowledge of the specific causes of behavior will eliminate the genesis of human suffering (*dukkha*), namely, desire (*taṇhā*) and ignorance (*avijjā*). Whereas a certain affinity between Buddhism and science is found in their view of an orderly structured, causally related, dynamic universe, the focal moral concern of Buddhism is lacking in the scientific view.

In recent years much excitement has been generated among Buddhists by the research of psychologists such as Ian Stevenson, at the University of Virginia, and Prof. Gilbert Rhine, of the Parapsychology Institute in Durham, North Carolina, not to mention such people as Edgar Cayce, founder of the Association for Research and Enlightenment at Virginia Beach. When the author was in Ceylon in 1967 he met a Ceylonese Buddhist medical doctor whose first question was, "What do you think of

Stevenson's book?" He was referring to Ian Stevenson's study of a number of case histories of people who had remembered previous existences. Some Buddhist apologists are convinced that there is now scientific verification from Western scholars to support the Buddhist theory of rebirth (*saṁsāra*). Francis Story (the Anagarika Sugatananda), a British convert to Buddhism, is especially committed to proving the scientific validity of the theory of rebirth and even made a tour of the United States in 1968 lecturing on this subject. In a booklet entitled *The Case for Rebirth* he traces a brief history of the belief in rebirth, going from ancient Egypt to the early church fathers and cabalistic Judaism to the contemporary interest in experiments in hypnotic regression. He contends that although some would dispute the grounds of rebirth as an explanation of the remembrance of previous existences, to account for all the testimonies now on record by means of telepathy, clairvoyance, or telekinesis it would be necessary to come up with a concept of "a freely-wandering, disembodied intelligence, independent of spatial and temporal limitations." [31] He goes on to say, "If we are to apply here the scientific law of parsimony, the more likely alternative is the obvious one that they are simply what they purport to be—memories of previous lives." [32]

The problem with the attempt to use science to prove or validate the truth of Buddhism (or for that matter, any religion) is rather obvious—the two are concerned with different kinds of truth. Scientific truth is public and observable while religious truth is private and subjective. Buddhism recognizes this distinction, as we have already noted, but among some apologists there is a tendency to forget it. To deal justly with their religion Buddhists should keep in mind Winston King's observation:

In the final analysis, it seems that religious experience and scientific experiment move on different levels and are only superficially to be called equivalent. In terms of basic attitudes, of the type of truth known, and of the materials involved, there is radical divergence. And it is better for both science and religion of whatever tradition to recognize this divergence. For the attempt to equate the two leads only to confusion.[33]

One final aspect of this problem, namely, Buddhist meditation, deserves special mention because of the importance it has played in the modern revival of Buddhism in Asia as well as the interest it has stirred in the West. We have mentioned that the practice of meditation might be likened to the laboratory of the scientist. It is that place where the individual, by his own efforts, tries to discover the Truth or the truth about existence. An even better comparison would be to say that meditation is the Buddhist equivalent of psychoanalysis in the West. It is an attempt on the part of the individual to probe the depths of his own being. One might contest this comparison by pointing out that in Buddhism meditation is used to test a priori assumptions about the nature of existence; however, who is to say that in certain forms of psychoanalysis there are not also some a priori assumptions made about the nature of human personality?

There are several ways in which the affinity between Buddhist meditation and psychoanalysis has been discussed. One is simply to analyze meditation from a psychoanalytic perspective. One Western Buddhist, a psychiatrist by training, describes the Buddhist notion of mindfulness (*sati*) of the three characteristics of existence (suffering, impermanence, and no-self) as gaining aware-

ness of those feelings, motives, and values which were
previously unconscious and, by bringing them into the
conscious arena, being able to deal effectively with them.[34]
Or, as Erich Fromm puts it, the main issue for both meditation and psychoanalysis is "the overcoming of repressed-
ness, the transformation of the unconscious into consciousness." [35] Some of the other affinities Fromm finds between
Zen meditation and psychoanalysis are: the fact that both
aim at ethical transformation, their insistence on independence from any kind of authority, and the similar
method of the psychoanalyst and the Zen meditation
master.[36]

Buddhist meditation has also been related to various
scientific studies, including sensory deprivation experiments
and electroencephalogram and energy metabolism tests.
Dr. Douglas M. Burns believes that sensory deprivation
facilitates awareness of emotional conflicts and thereby
abets personality growth in much the same way as does
Buddhist meditation.[37] A study of the medical and psychological aspects of Zen Buddhist meditation (*zazen*) was
conducted in Japan during 1961 and 1962, and for over
ten years Professor Kasamatsu of the Medical School,
Tokyo University, conducted an electroencephalographic
analysis of *zazen*. Some of the findings of these studies
were made into a 16mm. film entitled *The Science of
Zazen*. The main conclusion of the EEG study was that
the mental state of *zazen* veterans was such that it could
not be affected by either external or internal stimulus
beyond a mere response to it.[38] In this case a scientific
testing device was used to confirm the claims made by
the Zen tradition about the fruits of the practice of *zazen*.

In the face of the threat posed by hard-nosed scientific
attitudes, Buddhism may have as much to lose as the

religions of the West. Yet, Buddhism has its own kind of empiricism which insists that religious Truth cannot be given but only discovered by the efforts of every individual. Certainly Buddhism is not scientific in the modern, Western use of the term. But it does have within it an experimental, do-it-yourself individualism that may be especially appealing in today's world of increasing crisis.

BUDDHISM AS A WORLD RELIGION[39]

One of the curious paradoxes of our day is the juxtaposition of nationalism and internationalism. Asian Buddhism is nationalistically oriented in heritage and contemporary focus (see Chapter II) but is also very much involved in regional and international organizations. In some instances Buddhist internationalism is an obvious expression of its nationalistic perspective; in others, it is an attempt to promote greater cooperation among Buddhists or to contribute to an understanding of and solution to world problems. These two sides of the wider compass of contemporary Asian Buddhism are found in varying degrees in the concept of Buddhism as a world faith. Some of the aspects of this new vision of Buddhism that we shall examine are: the structures and message of "export Buddhism," Buddhism and world peace, and inter-Buddhist developments.

The term "export Buddhism" is one used by Winston King in referring in particular to the work of Western scholars interested in Buddhism or those who present Buddhist teachings to the West out of personal interest or conviction. We are using the term to refer to the recent interest on the part of Asian Buddhists to propagate their faith in the West. These efforts arose, in part, as King suggests, out of the fascination that Buddhism has had for Westerners. Mr. and Mrs. Rhys Davids, for example, were instrumental not only in founding the Pāli Text Society, which has been responsible for editing and translating the most important texts of Theravāda Buddhism, but also in supporting the Buddhist Society of Great Britain. A number of Europeans also emigrated to Buddhist Asia, where they made an important contribution to the understanding of Buddhism internationally. Ceylon, in particular, stands out in this regard as the adopted homeland of two English monks, Ñanamoli and Soma Thera, and of two German monks, Nyanatiloka and Nyanaponika Thera. The latter is one of the founder-editors of the Buddhist Publication Society.

The interest in developing Buddhist missions in the West has been particularly strong in Ceylon. In recent years Ceylonese Buddhists have supported missions in England (The London Buddhist Vihāra), West Germany (The Dhammadūta Society), and the United States (The Washington Vihāra) and in 1967 sent a Buddhist monk, The Venerable Piyadassi Thera, to Ghana. Laymen take great pride in the fact that their religion, which at one time was considered to be heathen by Christian missionaries from Europe, is now making an appeal in the West. The monk responsible for setting up the Washington Vihāra, The Venerable Vinitha Thera, has been particularly impressed with the reception he has received from American college students. On the basis of the response the Theravāda mission has received in the United States, the Washington Vihāra is planning to establish centers in the major metropolitan areas and train American bhikkhus to staff them. The first American Buddhists have already been selected for this task and are soon to begin a five-year training course in Ceylon. As yet the mission suffers from a lack of funds, but those directing it have high aspirations for the future.

One of the most important organizations in Ceylon for the propagation of Buddhism abroad is the Buddhist Publication Society. It was begun through the collaboration of three friends, two laymen and the German bhikkhu Nyanaponika Thera. It started with the intention of producing small booklets entitled *The Wheel* and tracts called *Bodhi Leaves* in English in order to reach a wide reading public around the world. By the end of its twelfth year of publication the BPS literature had been sent to addresses in seventy-one countries, and by May of 1969 over a million booklets had been printed. A Sinhalese series has also been started, and the Society's publications have been translated into nine foreign languages. The booklets are of a varied nature. They include translations of Pāli Suttas, scholarly studies of particular topics, and attempts "to present Buddhism in the framework of contemporary thought and to interpret man to himself in the light of a wisdom that is lacking in this materialistic age." [40]

Ceylon is not alone in its missionary zeal. Thailand also has a Dhammadūta Society for the purpose of training missionaries to be sent abroad, in particular to the West. Training includes language courses in a center equipped with a modern language lab. Thailand supports a temple and a meditation center in London led by The Venerable Chao Khun Phra Sobhana Dhammasudhi, an extremely able meditation teacher who has lectured in both Europe and North America.[41] It also supports the Washington Vihāra. In addition to the relatively small number of Theravāda Buddhist missions in America,

there are many Buddhist churches belonging to the Jodo
Shin Shu sect incorporated under the name The Buddhist
Churches of America. The first Jodo Shin Shu priests came
to America at the turn of the century, and at present
there are well over fifty congregations concentrated largely
in Hawaii and on the West Coast. Other Japanese Buddhist groups include the American Zen Institute founded
by Ruth Fuller Sasaki and an aggressively evangelic Soka
Gakkai mission with headquarters in Los Angeles. Of
particular relevance to our study at this point is the nature
of the appeal being made by "export Buddhism."

The most obvious claim is that the contemporary Buddhist apologetic is quite varied. Disregarding the in-
digenized Buddhist Churches of America, which are a
special case, one attraction of Buddhism is the practice of
meditation. At a time when the traditional religious disciplines of Judaism and Christianity (e.g., prayer) seem
irrelevant to many college students, the no-nonsense, do-
it-yourself approach of Zen is attracting a number of
followers who are not only from among the socially alienated. Soka Gakkai, a radical contrast to the quietistic Zen
approach, conducts *shakabuku*, evangelistic-type meetings,
all over the country with the simple message that faith
in Saint Nichiren and the Lotus Sutra will bring one
success and happiness. These meetings resemble a far-out
blending of pep rally and old-fashioned tent meeting. Of
greater importance than either the practice of Buddhist
meditation or the shock methods of Soka Gakkai are the
attempts to fashion a Buddhist apologetic offering Buddhism, of all the world's religions, as the most appropriate
for modern man. A few of the dominant themes of this
message are: the strong tradition of tolerance and peace
that has characterized Buddhism throughout the centuries;

the rational nature of Buddhism, especially the analytical and empirical foundations of Theravāda Buddhism; and Buddhism's emphasis on the individual, along with its nondogmatic, nonauthoritarian approach. Venerable Dr. Walpola Rahula, noted Buddhist author and vice-chancellor of Vidyodaya Buddhist University, has emphasized three fundamental appeals Buddhism has for all men: its moral and ethical aspect, especially its teachings on compassion and universal love; its intellectual and philosophical appeal, which stands for freedom of thought and inquiry; and its attitude toward social and economic problems, which will allow it to move toward a socialistic ideal.[42] In particular, Rahula advocates a Buddhism with a strong social commitment. He disagrees with the common misconception that to follow the Buddha's teaching means retirement from the world: "It may be agreeable for certain people to live a retired life in a quiet place. . . . But it is certainly more praiseworthy and courageous to practise Buddhism living among your fellow beings, helping them and being of service to them." [43]

Another aspect of the international appeal Buddhism is making deserving special mention is its emphasis on world peace. As we have already noted, Soka Gakkai affirms eternal world peace as the goal of its middle-of-the-road policy, and many Buddhist groups throughout Asia actively support international peace movements. The majority of contemporary writings on Buddhism and peace take the customary approach of focusing on correcting individual attitudes. For example, Soma Thera writes: "The whole spirit of the Buddha's teaching is one of pacification, patience and tolerance, and in the calm and placid atmosphere of this teaching there is every chance of reaching the destruction of violence within man. It is when the violence within men is destroyed that peace on earth can be securely established." [44] A notable exception to this traditionally Buddhist approach are the recent lectures on Buddhism's contribution to international law delivered by Prof. K. N. Jayatilleke of the University of Ceylon at The Hague during the summer of 1967.[45] These represent not simply an assertion that Buddhism does now and has always stood for peace but a closely reasoned, thoroughly documented effort to present the contribution Buddhism can make toward the development of a just and ordered world society. They are particularly significant as an example of an Asian Buddhist striving to make Buddhism relevant to the problems of man in the modern world.

One final aspect of Buddhism as a world religion to be mentioned is inter-Buddhist developments. The most important of these is the World Fellowship of Buddhists. It was founded in 1950 by Dr. G. P. Malalasakera in Colombo, Ceylon, with current headquarters in Bangkok, Thailand. There are regional centers all over Asia as well as in the West. A monthly News Bulletin carries information about international Buddhist activities. International conferences are held every two years at host countries in Asia. There was a period when they were overly politicized, especially in regard to the seating of delegations from mainland China and/or Taiwan. However, with the 1964 conference at Sarnath the decision was made to eliminate political issues from all business meetings and discussions.

It is difficult to gauge the significance of the World Fellowship of Buddhists. There is a tendency among critics to depict it as a peripheral organization with little or no effect. Such a judgment would be too harsh. The Fellowship has at least given Buddhism an international organization that brings into contact layman and monk from both Theravāda and Mahāyāna countries. That in itself is an important accomplishment. As Christmas Humphreys observed in connection with the Sarnath Conference, "Buddhist leaders of goodwill from thirty countries and all schools of Buddhism met in amity, prepared to understand the problems and achievements of other Centres, and to produce between them the beginnings of a reservoir of power which can be used as a force for world-wide understanding and hence world peace." [46]

There are a number of other events and organizations of importance that could be mentioned in relationship to Buddhism as a world religion, such as: the celebrations in connection with the Buddha Jayanti from 1954 to 1957, which greatly increased contact among Asian Buddhists; the growing movement back and forth of bhikkhus attending universities in Japan, India, Ceylon, and elsewhere; and the international Buddhist publications appearing, such as the monthly periodical World Buddhism, printed in Ceylon. Another ambitious undertaking is the formation of the World Sangha Council, with a permanent headquarters in Colombo. Hopes for the Council include greater understanding between Theravāda and Mahāyāna Buddhism, a more realistic assessment of the role of the Sangha in the light of new social and economic changes, and a new understanding and purification of Buddhist doctrine.[47] Whether or not these goals will be realized is an open question. At the very least the organizational structure has been provided for greater cooperation among the monastic organizations of Asian countries.

Buddhism as a world religion is not a new concept. Rather, it is part of the traditional understanding of Buddha Dhamma and was put into practice by King Aśoka, who is reputed to have sent missionaries not only to Ceylon, Burma, and other parts of Asia, but to the West as well. There is a sense, therefore, in which Buddhists feel they are simply beginning to realize what has always been a part of their religion. Many of their early efforts have been groping, misguided, or abortive but with time and experience there should be some improvements.

It cannot be denied that the form and even the content of Buddhism in Southeast Asia is being altered. To be sure, Buddhism in Ceylon, Burma, Thailand, and Vietnam is encrusted with traditional ideas and practices. For instance, magical animism is still a normative ingredient of much village Buddhism. Yet, monks are beginning to be trained in a variety of fields and are participating actively in social uplift, and laymen who might have been thoroughly secular two decades ago may now be seeking to apply the insights of meditation in their everyday lives. In short, Buddhism in Asia is not simply offering a static rehearsal of age-old patterns. As will be graphically illustrated in the following chapter, there are signs that in some countries a dynamic reformation of Buddhism may be taking place, offering the hope that Buddhism's own responsiveness will serve to enhance its ability to guide the sociocultural revolution of which it is inevitably a part.

IV

TWO PORTRAITS
OF THAI BUDDHISM

In Chapters II and III we have sketched descriptively the outline of a landscape picture of Buddhism in contemporary Southeast Asia. Even this one picture is far from complete and several others could have been drawn. In this chapter we shall offer two more sketches, but rather than sweeping landscapes we propose small portraits of two Thai monks, one illustrating both traditionalistic and modernistic aspects of the Sangha and the other depicting the most significant thinker within contemporary Thai Buddhism and a genuine innovator. By way of conclusion we shall evaluate all three pictures of Asian Buddhism in the light of the question—Asian Buddhism, resurgence or reformation?

PHRA MAHĀ SĪLA,
EDUCATIONAL ADMINISTRATOR

The hazy early-morning dawn is beginning to stretch over the Chao Phraya River as a small file of Buddhist monks starts out from Kalajaanmit temple (*wat*)[1] in Thonburi on their daily alms rounds. They will be out about an hour receiving rice, curries, and an occasional sweet from the pious followers of the Lord Buddha. This morning ritual provides sustenance for the Buddhist monk, or bhikkhu, as well as merit for the devout layman. It is one of the most important daily religious acts and points to the reciprocal nature of the relationship between monk and layman in Thailand.

Among the saffron-robed bhikkhus departing from Wat Kalajaanmit is Phra Mahā Sīla, who has taken his black, iron begging bowl on this same route morning after morning for nearly ten years. He had arisen an hour earlier to follow the custom of the Buddhist monastic life—that of performing his individual devotions in front of the Buddha altar in his small, one-room dwelling and of taking his morning bath before going outside the monastery. As he walks along the familiar, meandering streets his eyes are downcast and his face expressionless. His demeanor is unchanging, even when devout laymen ladle rice into his bowl. No smile of acknowledgment is necessary; both monk and layman are fulfilling their time-honored religious duties.

While Phra Mahā Sīla walks the streets of Thonburi, his mind, trained through years of practice, turns to reflect on the Mettā Sutta, one of the *paritta*, or mantric texts, used to ward off evil. Probably originating in Ceylon before the first century A.D., they have been incorporated into the *Royal Book of Chants* of Thailand and are used on various auspicious occasions (e.g., New Year's ceremonies, rain ceremonies).[2] On this particular morning, Phra Mahā Sīla is concentrating on the passage: "Let no one deceive another nor despise any person whatever in any place. . . . In anger or illwill let him not wish harm to anyone. . . . Let him cultivate a boundless heart towards all beings,"[3] as a means of mental purification. It is also, he thinks, a way to enhance the merit gained by those laymen who provide him with food.

Within half an hour the monk has been given enough rice to suffice for his two daily meals. Like all bhikkhus following the Theravāda *vinaya* (rules of discipline) he cannot consume any food after twelve noon. He had not expected to return to the temple so early, but one layman on his route was opening a new business and to ensure his success filled the monks' alms bowls almost to the brim.

Upon returning to the *wat*, Phra Mahā Sīla busies himself preparing his morning meal. He is served by a teen-age schoolboy from the country who in return for lodging at the monastery performs certain services for the monks and for the temple upkeep. Sometimes these *dek wat* (children of the temple) come from very poor families, with the temple assuming responsibility for them much as an orphanage might. Moreover, as is frequently the case in Bangkok and surrounding areas, many of these teen-agers use the temple monastery as a dormitory while studying at city schools.

Completing his simple meal of rice and curry, the bhikkhu has some time to rest before going to the *vihāra*[4] with the other monks and novices to chant the morning service. There are two daily ritual services in which all ordained members of the temple are expected to partici-pate—one after the morning meal and the other in the evening about dusk. The worship begins with the monks chanting obeisance to the Three Gems[5] (the Buddha, the Dhamma, and the Sangha) in front of a large, seated Buddha image and tiered altar on which are placed lighted candles, incense, flowers intricately woven into lotus buds, and a number of other venerated objects. Following the familiar Pāli words, *"namo tassa bhagavato arahato sammasambuddhassa*" (We worship the Blessed One, Arahant, Supreme Lord Buddha), the chants describe the nature of the Buddha, the grace of the Dhamma, and the virtue of the Sangha. Other stanzas remind the monks of the basic teachings of the Theravāda tradition—the characteristics of suffering (*dukkha*) and the impermanent (*anicca*), essenceless (*anatta*) nature of existence. Theravāda Buddhism teaches that until a person gains insight into the true nature of existence he has no hope of attaining ultimate salvation (Nibbāna).

On an ordinary day Phra Mahā Sīla and his colleagues are seated by themselves in the temple, but on the weekly Buddhist Sabbath Day (*wan phra*)[6] a congregation also attends the morning service. Women usually predominate in the relatively small congregation, although on festival occasions the compound will be crowded with men and women, both young and old. On *wan phra* after the chanting of the Pāli Suttas, the Eight Precepts are given to the congregation. On Sabbath Days lay Buddhists are enjoined to maintain a holy aloofness from the world: to refrain from killing, refrain from stealing, refrain from fornication, refrain from lying, refrain from intoxicating liquor, refrain from eating after the noon hour, refrain from dancing, singing, music, and entertainments, refrain from adorning the body with flowers, perfumes, or dyes, and from lying on high and wide beds.[7] Usually the abbot or other high-ranking monk will preach a sermon expositing the Dhamma. The sermon is read from a long, narrow palm-leaf or heavy paper text, although other and more extemporaneous styles may be used. At the conclusion of the service a *truat naam* ceremony may be held, where holy water is poured slowly into a bowl while the monks chant a blessing transferring the merit accrued by the worship to all living creatures.[8] The *truat naam* serves as a reminder that throughout Thai Buddhism traditional Theravāda forms are impregnated with extratraditional, archaic practices.

At the conclusion of the morning service Phra Mahā Sīla returns to his room to meditate and study. There was an earlier day when he would have gone to the temple school to be taught Buddhist history, doctrine, and monastic discipline. Indeed, the main purpose of coming to Bangkok from his home in Northeastern Thailand was to pursue his studies in the schools of the Buddhist Sangha. He had studied at the Pāli Training Schools in his own village and in the provincial center of Khon Kaen. After being ordained a novice (sāmaṇera) at the age of sixteen, he was sent to the Khon Kaen temple by his father, who did not have enough income from his small paddy holdings to send his son to government schools for further education.

The abbot of the Khon Kaen temple agreed to keep the young man and allow him to study in his school in exchange for performing certain housekeeping services around the temple and monastery grounds. The experience in Khon Kaen proved to be one of the turning points in Mahā Sīla's life. The abbot was one of those rare spirits who genuinely inspire those with whom they come into contact. Even though a strict disciplinarian, the abbot was also a serious student of Buddhist scripture and carefully tried to uphold the Buddhist vinaya. Finding in Phra Mahā Sīla a willing and able pupil, the abbot seized every opportunity to encourage him. Finally he sent the young man to Bangkok to complete his third level of naag tham[9] studies and to be ordained a bhikkhu at the traditional age of twenty-one.

For Phra Mahā Sīla, as for many other young men from the poorer areas of Thailand, the Sangha has been the

only means through which to secure advanced education.
Through its schools the monastic establishment provides
one of the principal avenues of social mobility and advancement. Not only did Phra Mahā Sīla complete his
naag tham studies through the Pāli Training Schools,
but in Bangkok he was admitted to Mahāchulalongkorn
Rājāvidylāya, the university for Buddhist monks of the
Mahānikāya, the largest of the two sects of Theravāda
monks in Thailand. Phra Mahā Sīla's studies at the
Mahānikāya university were completed in 1961 when he
was granted a Bachelor of Science degree in Buddhist
studies. Graduation from Mahāchulalongkorn was particularly fortuitous for Phra Mahā Sīla, for it meant an opportunity to study in India as part of a program under-
written by the Asia Foundation to train leaders of the
two Buddhist universities. He attended Benares Hindu
University from June of 1964 through May of 1967 and
earned a master's degree in ancient Indian history and
culture. When the monk returned to Thailand from
India he assumed the post of acting dean in the Faculty
of Humanities and Social Welfare at Mahāchulalongkorn
Rājāvidylāya.

With the morning service of worship concluded, Phra
Mahā Sīla settles himself at a desk crowded with books
in Pāli, Thai, and English. This particular morning the
volume that he has selected to read contains instructions
on breathing meditation, or mindfulness. Although the
monk has been more a student of Theravāda texts and
traditions than a practitioner of meditation, the disciplines of mindfulness (*sati*) and concentration (*samādhi*)
hold an inherent fascination for him. Those Buddhists
most intent on attaining Nibbāna practice meditation as
a means of controlling the body and the consciousness.
It is also a means to internalize and validate the more

psychological and philosophical descriptions of human existence described in the Abhidhamma texts.[10]

By eleven o'clock Phra Mahā Sīla has completed his reading and with the help of one of the young temple boys is served his noon and final meal of the day. One of his lay followers, a wizened but bright-eyed Chinese lady, has brought him a special treat of a pearlike fruit smothered in sweetened coconut milk. She sits to one side in a proper attitude of respect, occasionally cackling delightedly at the apparent relish with which the monk devours the proffered treat. After the meal, the bhikkhu has time for a short nap before leaving Wat Kalajaanmit to assume his responsibilities at Mahāchulalongkorn University as administrator and teacher of ancient Indian history and culture. It will be early evening before he can return.

Unlike Phra Mahā Sīla, many bhikkhus and sāmanera(s) (novices) have limited responsibilities. Although behavior varies from wat to wat as well as from individual to individual, the average monk leads a reasonably free and unscheduled life. Some monks take advantage of their freedom and become rather lazy and indifferent. However, as many observers have commented, life within the wat frequently exemplifies a continuing pace of activities and duties.[11] One student of Thai village life backs up his claim that life in a village wat is not an idle one by a detailed schedule of the daily activities of the monks and novices.[12] Much of the novices' time may be taken up in study and memorization of Pāli chants to be used in a variety of ritual services. Correspondingly, a number of monks in a particular temple may be involved in teaching. In addition to the duties of study and teaching, monks and novices will perform a variety of responsibilities around the temple compound.

The activities of the monks are characterized by both monastic and social aspects. One observer of Thai village Buddhism has noted that the organized daily behavior of the monks and novices tends to emphasize the monastic aspect of their role, whereas the weekly pattern of behavior is more social in orientation.[13] Both aspects of the monk's role are part of the centrality of the *wat* in village life which is the most active and viable social unit beyond the family.[14] The crucial role played by the *wat* in most of rural Thailand is illustrated by the following functions the *wat* performs in the community: counseling agency, community center, hospital, school, community chest, free hotel, news agency, charity employment center, morgue, music school, reservoir, and home for the aged.[15]

The importance of the temple and the monastic community is furthered by the monks' leadership in a wide variety of religious and social ceremonies. Of those which center about the life cycle, the most important is the funeral rite. It is an elaborate ceremony and may involve the outlay of considerable sums of money. Ordinary funerals in northern Thailand may last over a period of three days.[16] A funeral attended by the author in Bangkok began at nine A.M. and lasted until after five P.M. The morning activities were primarily for the family of the deceased and included a sermon dwelling on the theme of the transience of life, chanting of Pāli Suttas for the benefit of the deceased and the presentation of food and gifts to the monks. The afternoon service was primarily for the invited guests, who paid their respects by placing incense sticks, candles, and flowers before the coffin prior to the actual cremation. The atmosphere at a Buddhist funeral seems almost festive. Where funerals last over a three-day period the neighbors gather nightly to feast, play games, and gossip.[17] During a typical funeral in Bangkok, a Thai band may be playing during most of the day. Guests invited to the afternoon service are served soft drinks and offered cigarettes. Seated before the crematorium in an area shaded by awnings for the occasion, guests will use the opportunity to talk about matters of business or family and greet old friends they have not seen for some time.

Also, monks will be called upon to take part in a variety of predominantly Brahman-animistic festivals centering about the home and the agricultural community. Among the most important of these are housewarming rites, the erection of spirit houses, and the ritual of first plowing. Bhikkhus will be involved in these festivals in a variety of ways. For example, in the ceremony of first plowing the abbot of the local temple may be called upon to play the role of astrologer and to set the time, day, and week of the occasion. This particular role is not an unusual one for a Buddhist monk to perform. In fact, many monks are noted not only for their astrological skills but for a variety of magical arts. Some may gain a reputation for making holy water especially efficacious in the healing of diseases. Others practice the art of fortune-telling. Even though these activities are specifically prohibited in the Pāli canon, monks are still allowed and sometimes encouraged to practice them. Some *wats*, however, do not permit monks to practice such arts as fortune-telling since they are specifically disavowed by the Theravāda scriptures.

In the early evening Phra Mahā Sīla finishes his work at Mahāchulalongkorn Buddhist University and returns to Wat Kalajaanmit. His temple has had a long history, going back to King Rama III (1824–1851). It gradually

altered in character as the population around the *wat*
shifted from a Thai to a predominantly Chinese grouping.
In front of the large image of the Buddha in the posture
of subduing Mara has been placed a smaller image of the
Amida Buddha, the Lord of the Pure Land and the principal Buddha of the Chinese Mahāyānists in Bangkok.
The temple itself is still Theravāda, but as Mahā Sīla
observes, many Chinese people come to the temple with
the aspirations and attitudes typical of Mahāyāna Buddhism. Also, in front of the entrance to the temple are
to be found images of Chinese deities that are rendered
special worship on such occasions as Chinese New Year.
It is an interesting aspect of Thai Buddhism that Mahāyāna forms are not necessarily restricted to the few
Chinese and Vietnamese temples located predominantly
in the Bangkok area. Thai Buddhism is an eclectic synthesis of various forms of Buddhism, animism, and Brahmanism.

Phra Mahā Sīla has returned to his temple just in time
to take part in the evening service. The monks and novices file quietly in and take their places before the image
of the Buddha. Mahā Sīla's day has been a busy one
filled with many problems confronting Buddhist education as it attempts to become contemporary in a day of
rapid change. He has had little time for meditation and
reflection so he appreciates this time together with his
saffron-robed colleagues. Together they pay homage to
their enlightened teacher and pledge to serve him. Their
chanting echoes into the quiet Thonburi night: "I beg
to be the servant of the Lord Buddha, he is my Lord and
master. The Lord Buddha has banished suffering and has
given me benefits and help. My body and my life I offer
to the Lord Buddha and will follow him." [18]

BUDDHADĀSA BHIKKHU, "STREAM-WINNER," REFORMER

He hardly looks like a "Stream-winner (*sotāpanna*), the first of four levels of sanctification on the way to the realization of Nibbāna. He is overweight, and his robes look like rejects from the local Chinese cloth merchant. But there are Buddhists in Thailand who call Buddhadāsa a saint. Some claim he is the most outstanding Buddhist thinker in the country, while others tried to oust him from the Sangha a few years ago by claiming he was a Communist. He is anything but an ordinary bhikkhu. The son of a well-to-do merchant in southern Thailand, he decided at the age of twenty-one to enter the Sangha, not an unusual step for a Thai male. What followed was unusual, however. After finishing the traditional levels of monastic study and teaching for a short time, he retired to the forest for a period of six years to meditate and to study the Pāli texts. He is reputed to have adopted a life of complete isolation, even to the point of having his brother leave food hanging from a tree in order to avoid the human contact that is part of the monk's traditional morning begging rounds. He returned to the "world" and was eventually made abbot of Wat Phradhatu in Chaiya, South Thailand, a temple associated with the extension of the Sumatran-based Shrivajaya Kingdom in the eighth century A.D. Yet, he was not happy in this role, and for the past decade has focused his energy on the establishment of a forest hermitage about four kilometers outside Chaiya.

The hermitage is called, appropriately enough, "Garden of Liberation" (Suan Mok). Here Buddhadāsa has built a center that expresses his concern for a Buddhism reflect-

ing the essential teachings of the Buddha in a manner
relevant to a world of mass media communication. In a
way, Suan Mok is a contradiction in terms. It represents,
to the degree that it is possible, an original Buddhism designed with a sensitivity to the modern context in which
it finds itself. There are simple, single, wooden dwelling
places for nearly forty monks set in the midst of a lovely
forest together with two modern buildings, a museum-
library and a "spiritual theater." The inside of the latter
is covered with a variety of paintings from Theravāda
and Mahāyāna traditions as well as other religions. Set
in the outside walls are a number of bas-reliefs reproduced
from structures at the early Indian Buddhist centers of
Sanchi, Bharhut, and Amaravati. When completed, the
building will also serve as a lecture hall and theater for
the teaching of Buddhism through a variety of audio-
visual aids.

Through the artwork in the theater Buddhadāsa tries
to convey the essential elements of Buddhism—existence
in the world is characterized by attachment, attachment
produces suffering, suffering is overcome only when we
are freed from the acquisitiveness of self. The two principal themes Buddhadāsa elaborates as he guides a person
through the theater is the nature and consequence of attachment to the world of things and the higher goal to
which Buddhism points the way. Surprisingly enough,
the Pāli term used most by Buddhadāsa to describe that
goal is *suñña*, or the Void, symbolized by a huge white
circle, which dominates the hall. *Suñña* is not a negative
concept but represents that very real and positive state of
Being which Buddhism holds out as the goal of the salvation quest. As the Void, or Emptiness, it represents the
opposite of a condition of attachment to objects. It is
objectless, beyond all the polarities and distinctions that

characterize our mundane world of ordinary levels of understanding. The ultimate reality of Buddhism, as of every other religion, contends Buddhadāsa, is beyond human verbalization. Like many a Christian mystic as well as Indian and Chinese sage, he asserts that the ultimately real is beyond conceptualization. This theme is expressed in many of the early Indian bas-reliefs used by Buddhadāsa. In them one finds a consistent refusal to anthropomorphize the Buddha in recognition of his insistence that he was not to become an object of attachment. Nothing, not even the great teacher himself, can be venerated as ultimate reality.

The extensive use of the earliest forms of Buddhist art in India emphasizes the particularity of the Buddha, his genuine teachings, and the beginnings of the tradition. Buddhadāsa contends that many of the later developments within Buddhism are extraneous or even antithetical to the genuine teachings and intention of the Buddha. It must be recognized, he insists, that even the Pāli canon is a later extension of the earliest tradition. He is especially critical of those Theravāda teachers who would make the much venerated Abhidhamma literature normative for orthodox Theravāda belief. "They climb the tree of Buddhism from the top down," he says. Likewise he is a consistent critic of many of the teachings and practices within Thai Buddhism, ranging from the practice of fortune-telling by Buddhist monks to an undue emphasis on a physical interpretation of *kamma* and *samsāra*.[19]

Buddhadāsa's concern for the integrity of the particularity of genuine Buddhism is matched by his conviction of its universal truth. The fundamental problem of human existence is attachment, which leads to pride, selfishness, and egoism. Since religion's basic concern is with human existence, it must aim to solve the problem of attachment. The Buddha set out to accomplish this task. He discovered and taught a way to salvation, a new life characterized by nonattachment and freedom. It is a way to a new state of being in which one lives the ultimately real. Buddhism, affirms Buddhadāsa, is untrue to itself when it fails to teach the universal truth that its founder intended to be taught. Buddhadāsa finds this truth expressed in a variety of forms not all limited to Theravāda Buddhism. In particular, he has a profound appreciation for certain aspects of Mahāyāna Buddhism. He has translated some Mahāyāna Sutras into Thai, employs both Japanese and Chinese art in his spiritual theater, and will even use Zen koans as part of his meditation instruction.

Bhikkhu Buddhadāsa seems to make two basic assumptions regarding religion, the first being related to the purpose or intention of religion. Religion, in Buddhadāsa's view, is primarily a means or a way to salvation. It is redemption from one mode of existence and rebirth into a new one, release from suffering and sin and the experience of a new freedom and peace, overcoming attachment to the world through knowledge of the truth about the nature of things, and the release that results from shattering the bonds of preoccupation with the Self or the Ego. All these phrases are expressions of the same fundamental, redemptive purpose of religion qua religion. Hence, religion is not primarily an ethic, a philosophy, or a psychology, and to understand it as such is to discredit it. In this connection Buddhadāsa is sharply critical of those who would intellectualize Buddhism by claiming that it appeals to modern man on the grounds that Buddhism is a philosophy and not a religion. In his view, to the degree that a religion fails to fulfill its intended redemptive purpose, to that degree it fails to be a religion and becomes something else, e.g., ethics, philosophy, magic.

Contrary to a typical Western misinterpretation of Theravāda Buddhism, Bhikkhu Buddhadāsa does not think the redemptive process in Buddhism demands a literal withdrawal from the world. As he states in *People in Relation to Dhamma—Dhamma in Relation to People*, the Dhamma was not propounded in order to give people an excuse to escape from the world.[20] Buddhism, rather, helps men to live in the midst of the world of suffering while not being subject to suffering,[21] a theme that sounds very much like the familiar phrase, "to be in the world but not of it." The purpose of Buddhism is not to negate the world but to be freed from the suffering that characterizes the world. Because suffering is overcome, one has a new lease on life and experiences a new freshness and resilience.[22]

Bhikkhu Buddhadāsa's second assumption concerns the nature of the religious man who is suspended between the tension of the mundane and the transmundane, the profane and the sacred. Because of his existential dialectic, man's redemption, in its simplest but most profound form, is liberation from the mundane or the profane. The basic purpose of religion, then, is to resolve the tension between the polarities of the mundane and the transmundane or, in other words, to realize the ideal while being part of or participating in the actual. Until this resolution takes place, however, religious men and religious traditions are caught between the two poles.

This particular understanding of the nature of the religious life lies behind Buddhadāsa's extensive use of two categories, *phasaa khom* and *phasaa tham*, or "ordinary language" and "Dhamma language." *Phasaa khon* represents the mundane or empirical level, the level of religious understanding and discourse of the common man who lacks profound religious understanding. *Phasaa tham* stands for the transempirical level attained by the man of deep insight into the nature of things. This distinction is important for several reasons. It is, for instance, a device by which Buddhadāsa criticizes many popular misconceptions within Buddhism. In a book entitled *Handbook for Man*, he attacks those Buddhists who understand the principal purpose of their religion to be the performance of particular ceremonies rather than the elimination of suffering by coming to a knowledge of the truth about the nature of things.[23] Rites and rituals so misconstrued only serve to obstruct the true meaning of Buddhism. In an even more radical vein, he insists that the most fundamental concepts of Buddhism, such as Buddha, Dhamma, and Sangha, may become blocks to one's true religious quest.[24] When these "Three Gems" become "refuges" by which one hides from the realities of existence, they must be cast aside.

The categories of *phasaa khon* and *phasaa tham* are more than a means employed by Buddhadāsa to criticize particular ideas and practices within Thai Buddhism. They also function as the principal method by which he compares Buddhism and Christianity. On the level of *thama*, or Dhamma, he discusses many similarities between various concepts central to Christianity and Buddhism. "Eternal life" and "concentration" (*samādhi*) are likened to having a "strong heart"; the Golden Rule and *kamma* are related to each other through the notion of the reciprocity of deeds.[25] His analysis of the God concept in Christianity is especially interesting. On the level of Dhamma, Buddhadāsa asserts that the idea of

God is a concept essentially beyond the understanding of men and, therefore, transcends our usual distinctions between good and evil, personal and impersonal.[26] In Buddhadāsa's view, Christians must recognize that their ordinary, anthropomorphized conception of God is but a *phasaa khon* rendering of ultimate reality. Once this admission is made, then the Christian concept of God may be likened to Dhamma, the central concept in Theravāda Buddhism. The notions of God and Dhamma are both ultimate and universal. They are beyond the relativities of time and space; hence, in essence, both of these terms represent ultimate reality. Dhamma is fundamentally another term for Nature or the true nature of things. Similarly, to know God is to know things as they really are, or from the perspective of the divine (i.e., *phasaa tham*).

Bhikkhu Buddhadāsa's use of the categories *phasaa khon* and *phasaa tham*, based on his understanding of the religious man suspended between the mundane and the transmundane, has important consequences for his approach to interreligious dialogue. It allows him to discuss similarities between Buddhism and Christianity without identifying or amalgamating the two. Buddhadāsa is neither a syncretist nor a naïve idealist in his approach to interreligious dialogue. He contends that this endeavor can bear fruit only when religious men recognize the fact that they face the same human dilemma and share similar divine aspirations.

Shifting to a study of his method of understanding religion, we might characterize Buddhadāsa as an existentialist for whom the life of the religious man is of focal significance. In Thailand, Buddhadāsa has gained the reputation of being a revolutionary or an iconoclast be-

cause of his disdain for many elements absorbed into the
system or structure of Thai Buddhism. He insists that the
religious life is, above all, a salvation quest, and that every
religious expression, at its heart, must be part of this
quest. When the salvation orientation of a religion is dis-
torted by focusing on unnecessary and often superstitious
particulars within a religious tradition, its uniqueness as a
way of life is destroyed. His approach to religion is sup-
plemented by a type of phenomenological orientation.
That is, he takes particular religious phenomena and inter-
prets them in terms of broader categories, or higher levels
of understanding. In this way particular aspects of different religious traditions may be related without being
identified. This method can be illustrated by referring
again to Buddhadāsa's discussion of the God concept.

The concept of a personal God in Christianity is an
idea uniquely developed within the Christian tradition.
In order to be able to relate this concept to something
within Buddhism, Buddhadāsa describes the Christian
concept of a personal God in terms of the broader or
more abstract category of ultimate reality. By this method,
the notion of God is seen as a particular conceptualization
of the ultimately real, which is essentially beyond definition. Buddhadāsa does not argue that Christians should
eliminate the concept of a personal God, but he thinks
they should acknowledge that this concept is only one
way ultimate reality might be conceived. By this method
the God notion can then be related to the Buddhist
term "Dhamma," which is also taken as a particular
representation of ultimate reality.

Bhikkhu Buddhadāsa applies this methodology not only
to Christianity or to Buddhism in relationship to Christianity but to Buddhism per se. He demonstrates the

cogency of this approach in terms of such focal Theravāda doctrines as the Four Noble Truths and the concepts of *kamma* and *saṁsāra*. *Saṁsāra* is interpreted as pointing to a "new birth" in which one is freed from preoccupation with the self rather than as the customarily understood sequence of physical rebirths.[27] *Kamma*, rather than being conventionally described as the moral law of cause and effect, is interpreted as describing a condition of causal bondage beyond which Buddhism points the way.[28] The most provocative example of this approach, however, is Buddhadāsa's delineation of the essence of Buddhism. In effect, it is a reinterpretation of the Four Noble Truths.[29] Because Dhamma in Buddhadāsa's understanding is the nature of things, or the ultimately real, the Four Noble Truths are rendered as: (1) *Nature*, that which changes and that which does not, is devoid of essence; (2) the *law of nature* is that we are attached to things and, thereby, experience suffering; (3) our *duty* in the face of this fact is to act in such a way as to be freed from the results of our actions; (4) as a *result*, our life in this world will be happy and free from worry, because we have no attachment to things as "mine." [30] The Dhamma interpreted in terms of these categories represents a generalized stimulus to Buddhist thought and helps break down the isolation of traditional Buddhist terminology.

Buddhadāsa's method of understanding religion has been characterized as existential and phenomenological. It might be well to apply another label—demythological. As a demythologizer he looks for nonliteral levels of meaning in the mythological forms of a religious tradition. Hence, in the Genesis creation myth he takes one of the purposes of the Adam and Eve story to be a de-

scription of the nature of the relationship between man
and woman (Gen. 2:20 ff.). He also rightly asserts that
the discrepancy between the Genesis creation story and
the account of modern science is inconsequential, because the story is not a scientific account but an illustration of the spiritual truth that man is only fully man in
relationship to God.

Buddhadāsa's intellectual brilliance is matched by his
concern for the health and well-being of Thai Buddhism.
His practical innovations, intellectual perspicacity, and
spiritual sincerity perhaps earn for him the title *sotāpanna*.

Asian Buddhism: Resurgence or Reformation?

The question to which we must now address ourselves
is whether the modern revival of Buddhism in Southeast
Asia is primarily a resurgence of a historic religious tradition with little significant change or whether the revival
is also accompanied by genuine reformation. Or, in terms
of the question raised in the Introduction, is the response
of Asian Buddhism to the changes brought about by
technological modernity one of real engagement, capitu-
lation, or isolation? What signs are there that Asian Buddhism is retaining its identity but also its relevance to its
cultural society? In other words, is Asian Buddhism participating in Bellah's category of "creative tension" with
the world?

As we have seen there is no unequivocal answer to this
question, just as there would be no clear-cut answer were
it to be asked of religion in America. Perhaps by way of
comparison, it would be a fair generalization to say that
for both sociological and philosophical reasons, Asian
Buddhism faces more serious problems in this area than

religion in America. Although we do not subscribe to the opinion that Theravāda Buddhism is a religion of world denial or withdrawal, in comparison to Christianity its ontology and ethics provide less of a justification for world-transforming activity. On the other hand, they may provide a better perspective from which to raise critical questions about the direction of social, economic, and political change. It depends on whether a new impulse has taken place from within to give Buddhism the vitality necessary to reorient and redirect itself.

Ceylon, Burma, Thailand, Cambodia, Vietnam, and Japan have been mentioned in the course of this survey. The role of the Sangha and the laity in the rise of nationalism, the throes of traditional cultures being bombarded by Western scientific technology, patterns of education, values and mores, and the emergence of Asian nations into a world community have been some of the problems discussed. Clearly, Buddhism has not remained static in the face of changes that have taken place. The Sangha has acted as a strong political force in Burma, Vietnam, and also Ceylon, and laymen's associations have shown political muscle in Japan and Ceylon. We have looked at some of the attempts to fashion a viable social ethic in the face of changing social patterns and economies working toward more and more productivity, seen Buddhist monks studying sociology and being trained in community development, been somewhat bemused by attempts to justify Buddhist concepts scientifically, and noted the interest of Buddhists in projecting a worldwide image through such organizations as the World Fellowship of Buddhists. On occasion the Buddhist response to modernity and change has been adamantly resurgent rather than articulative of renaissance; however, the real

meaning of the picture we have sketched lies in particular
countries and situations, in the efforts being made by individuals like Mahā Sīla and Buddhadāsa toward shaping
a new, contemporaneous Buddhism. Who knows what
results the Ceylon Farmers' Association will produce? Or
the community development training programs in Thailand? The returns of projects such as these are too meager
to allow us to do more than make some predictions.

On the negative side, we can agree with those scholars
who contend that U Nu's Buddhism was too traditional
and that the legislation to make Buddhism the state
religion of Burma might not only have been politically
unfeasible but unfortunate for Burmese Buddhism as
well. In Ceylon, where the revival of Buddhism has been
led predominantly by lay Buddhist associations of the
educated elite, the direction has been overly traditionalistic and moralistic. Consequently it seems to be moving
more toward a reiteration of past values than toward offering a strong, dynamic reinterpretation of Buddhism in
the light of the present. Institutional and doctrinal reformation is often recommended, although actual changes
have not kept pace. The traditionalism in the revival of
Ceylonese Buddhism is reflected not only in the lack of a
dynamic, creative tension with society but also in a negative orientation or bias. We have noted that this bias has
expressed itself in a moralistic emphasis. It has also been
inextricably a part of an anti-Western value system, anti-
colonial and anti-Christian attitude. The Roman Catholics, in particular the Catholic Action Movement, have
been the subject of bitter attack.[31] In certain instances
the attack was justified and important correctives to situations unfairly and artificially created during Ceylon's colonial past have been affected. An essentially negative
stance, however, and militant reassertion of the rights of

Buddhism severely inhibit a creative interaction not only with other religious bodies in Ceylon but with serious social problems as well.

Despite the inadequacies of Buddhism in the nation-building process in Ceylon, Burma, and other Asian countries in the modern period, the possibilities of the development of a national ideology in which Buddhism plays a major role are significant. It is doubtful that making Buddhism the state religion, especially in religious and racially pluralistic societies, offers a very attractive option. If, however, one accepts the premise that Buddhism has been one of the most important forces in forming the world view of the majority of people in Ceylon, Burma, Thailand, Vietnam, or even Japan, it is both logically and practically sound to insist that Buddhist principles should have some normative function in various aspects of the social, political, and economic realms. An eloquent spokesman for this position is Prof. K. N. Jayatilleke, chairman of the Department of Philosophy at the University of Ceylon, Peradeniya. He has suggested, for example, that the legal system of Ceylon should not be based on a British model but "on Buddhist conceptions of justice after a careful study of the several systems operative in the world." [32] He is convinced that any socio-political system which slavishly imitates a Western model is bound to fail. Furthermore, he contends that if an indigenous ideology is not put into effect by competent and dedicated political leaders, then a Marxist revolution in countries like Ceylon will have a much greater chance of success.

Although this position is appealing, it contains an inherent danger, especially in the light of the conservative nature of the Buddhist resurgence in Asia and in view of the many internal problems that organized Buddhism itself faces. The danger is illustrated by a suggestion Professor Jayatilleke himself makes that an Institute of Buddhist Studies be established to advise the government of Ceylon about "matters on which the Buddhist point of view must be known before policies can be enunciated." [33] He likens the role of this institute to that of the Institute of Islamic Studies and Research in Pakistan.[34] The possibility posed by Professor Jayatilleke's proposal is precisely that suggested by his analogy, since Pakistan was created for the very purpose of becoming a religious state. Would such a formally structured Buddhist approach to a wide variety of problems inevitably lead to a *de jure* state religion? Given the nature of the Buddhist resurgence in Ceylon or even elsewhere in Southeast Asia, would it be possible to develop an ideology based on the broadly humanitarian and universalistic values of Buddhism without succumbing to the pressures of making Buddhism the state religion and thereby creating almost insuperable problems?

Before Buddhism can offer the kind of leadership that Asia needs in this transitional period, it must yet undergo a more sweeping reformation. In Ceylon, influential laymen have recommended many changes within the Sangha, and yet such changes, even when they do come about, are not enough in and of themselves. Structural innovations must not only be corrective of old ills but reflect the essential insights of Buddhism as well as the deep needs of a society. If the Sangha is basically concerned about its status, as apparently it was in Burma and still is today with the majority sect (Siyam) in Ceylon, the sorts of change liable to take place will impede and misguide social progress and, in the long run, condemn Buddhism to irrelevance.

Buddhism in Asia needs reformers like Buddhadāsa who are willing to take seriously one of the central tenets of Buddhism—that change is the very nature of things. No structure is permanent, least of all the Buddhist establishment. How well the author remembers a walk to the Buddhist "temple" at Buddhadāsa's forest hermitage. There was nothing but a shaded hilltop. As we left it, Buddhadāsa asked rhetorically, "Why should large sums of money be expended on beautiful temples when times have changed and such structures no longer fulfill the role they once did?" "Nothing," he said, "can become an object of attachment, not a temple, not even the Buddha himself." The essence of Buddhism places it on the cutting edge of change but in such a way that change itself is transcended. Buddhism acknowledges the necessity of change and at the same time is critical of it. What better perspective could be found to aid modernity in Asia!

Of all the particular developments within Asian Buddhism that have been mentioned, the ones that hold the greatest promise are the new roles being assumed by monks and laymen. Lay associations made a valuable contribution to independence movements in a number of Asian countries and have encouraged reforms within the Sangha. Monks themselves are demanding a wider educational experience and are preparing to make a greater contribution to social development. Monks and laymen are also participating together in such organizations as the World Fellowship of Buddhists. These new roles offer a greater opportunity for mutual influence, thereby serving to break down the traditional barriers that tended to separate the bhikkhu and the layman.

An Asian Buddhist observing the American religious

scene today would be as hard pressed as we are to come
up with a set of valid generalizations about religion and
change, especially in attempting to answer the question
at hand. He probably would note that the greatest religious revival in modern America was the decade following
World War II, and that in the decade of the '60s interest in organized religion was on the decline. Perhaps
he would even speculate about the reasons for this decline, concluding that American religion had become an
institutional establishment that had aborted its proper
function by surrendering the creative tension between
religion and its cultural society. Here is the greatest danger Asian Buddhism faces today—that in its search for
status it will abrogate the place of creative tension with
its cultural society. That will happen if it sells out to
change, as some political bhikkhus have done, or if it
ignores it, as some pious, well-meaning lay leaders have
done. In either case, Buddhism will sacrifice its creative
tension with its cultural society.

> When everything has been said and done, it is only
> a new religious impulse from within the religion
> concerned that can give the process of reorientation
> and redirection a new and real vitality. . . . It is
> . . . only through the spiritual agony engendered
> by facing the crisis of the times and through reach-
> ing from the depths of one's own religious experi-
> ence that it becomes possible to reaffirm and restate
> one's religion's essential relationship with society
> and to reintegrate the moral forces impelling the
> convulsive changes of our time into the living cen-
> ter of one's religion.[35]

V

BUDDHISM AND THE WEST

In the preceding chapters we have focused our attention on a selective description and analysis of Buddhism in Southeast Asia. Yet, if one could prognosticate the future, it might well be predicted that a significant dimension of a Buddhist renaissance will take shape not in Asia but in the West. There are evidences to this effect already. Most students of Japanese Buddhism, for instance, contend that the interest in Zen Buddhism in America stimulated by the English writings of D. T. Suzuki has been partially responsible for a renewed interest in Zen in Japan. Furthermore, as noted in Chapter III, there is an increasing effort among various Theravāda and Mahāyāna groups to propagate Buddhism in the West. Such efforts must inevitably mean that Buddhism, in reacting to different cultural situations, will be called upon to divest itself of some of the excess cultural baggage in which it has become encrusted. Consequently, the stimulus Buddhism receives in the West may mean a renewed appreciation for what Mrs. Rhys Davids fondly referred to as "the

original Gospel of **Buddhism**" freed from extraneous ac-
cretions.

The author has been witness to just such a phenomenon. In January of 1969 and 1970, workshops in Buddhist
meditation were conducted at Oberlin College. To lead
the project, a Thai meditation teacher, The Venerable
Chao Khun Sobhana Dhammasudhi, was invited from
England, where since 1964 he has been the head priest
of the Buddhapadīpa Temple in London. Operating in an
American college context, the monk was called upon to
interpret the essentials of Buddhism in an intelligible and
meaningful manner to college students. The central message of Buddhism, rather than losing meaning, was enhanced. Its highest goals and ideals were appreciated and
understood in some instances, perhaps, even more genuinely than among those who call themselves Buddhist.
One student in the workshop wrote the following description of his experience, a description that points to a keen
perception of the essential thrust of Buddhism:

> Improvisation on a musical instrument is an activity
> made possible by the mind's apprehension of the vi-
> brations that occur between accident and plan. In
> some sense this might be a description of any event
> or experience of the human condition; I find it ap-
> propriately analogous to my personal meditation ex-
> periences of last month. For I cannot speak of reali-
> zations and discoveries as meaningful intellectual
> events in the sense in which I would have intended
> these words a month ago. In fact it is the very dis-
> tinction between description and intellectualization
> that has been dissolved, so that any real understand-
> ing of events around and within the residence of
> what I call my consciousness can only stand in terms

of experiential activities. Absolutely anything and everything might be anticipated by the imagination; yet an actual event is simply the merging of the infinite with the infinitesimal.

Three experiences stand out in my mind that occurred in the first two weeks, practicing Theravāda meditation. On the third day I was meditating alone in the evening, attempting awareness over impermanence. Following the arising, existing, and passing away of each individual breath, I achieved for a period of time a balance between mindfully perceiving this impermanence and that of the pain of the full lotus position. . . . In this manner I sank deeper into a state of conscious active peace. Suddenly I became aware of loud shouts and laughter in the hall outside my room; then came sounds of people running, and a door slammed; and silence was again as before. In this event was a realization of the object of meditation in the three worlds before me at that instant, and as I became the utter truth of impermanence of noise, breathing, and pain, that self-conscious seer was no more.

Among American college students at this time there is an active and increasing interest in Asian religions. While acknowledging the esoteric appeal of Buddhism and other Asian religions, this interest is not simply part of the youthful rebellion against the religious establishment. Rather, much student involvement in these areas reflects a genuine quest for a meaningful set of values and a viable life-style. Nor is the growing interest in Buddhism simply the preserve of the young. John Cobb, an outstanding contemporary theologian, has observed that Buddhism offers one of the most compelling religious alternatives today,[1] and Christian ministers utilizing Buddhist insights and practices are becoming less and less rare. Indeed, a United Church minister friend of mine recently wrote requesting information on Zen Buddhism to be used in a senior high church school class.

In this country we are faced with an increasingly open and pluralistic religious situation. It offers the kind of dynamic circumstances in which Buddhism, of all the historic non-Western religions, will have to be taken more and more seriously. As we have observed, the face of Buddhism will undoubtedly be somewhat altered in the process. Yet, the consequences for religion in the West may also be profound. We shall now examine this interesting problem by focusing on the "dialogical" approach of Wilfred Cantwell Smith, the "appreciative" encounter of Thomas Merton, the "appropriative" attitude of Alan Watts, and finally by offering some preliminary suggestions of our own.

BUDDHISM AND CHRISTIANITY IN DIALOGUE

Certainly a significant part of the Buddhist-Christian encounter in the West and the East will involve a mutual understanding and respect among religious persons. In the past the attitude of Christians toward Buddhism and other non-Christian religions has often been one of suspicion or disagreement. Even where a sympathetic view has been taken by Christian scholars there has sometimes been either an implicit or an explicit attitude of the superiority of Christianity. Such a position, for example, seems to be represented by R. C. Zaehner, Spalding Professor of Eastern Religion and Ethics at the University of Oxford. Zaehner is critical of those who would try to pinpoint the differences between Christianity and non-Christian religions. He claims to try to bridge the gap between them and says, "We must seek to understand them [i.e., non-Christian religions] from within and try to grasp how they too seek to penetrate the mystery of our being and our eternal destiny." [2] Certainly Zaehner's treatises on comparative religions and interreligious encounter display a profound knowledge of non-Christian religious traditions as well as a sympathetic understanding of them.

Zaehner's approach is characterized by two primary traits: finding parallels between the Christian tradition and other religious traditions, and seeing Christianity as the fulfillment or consummation of all other religions. In his analysis of the Indian religious tradition, for example, he is quick to see similarities between the Upanishadic description of the relationship between the soul and God (Chāndogya 3.14) and the thought of the modern Roman Catholic mystic Thomas Merton. More telling, however, is Zaehner's treatment of Indian theism. In the triumph of Krishna devotion in the Bhagavad Gītā and the sequence of Krishna's life in the Mahabharata, he sees a reminder "of the passion, Resurrection and Ascension of Our Lord." [3]

Despite Zaehner's efforts to bridge the gap between Christianity and the Indian religious tradition by means of parallels, in the last analysis he is unwilling to treat the two religions as equals. Hence, the message of Krishna in the Bhagavad Gītā "is the message that Christ was later to proclaim in its fullness." [4] In what is perhaps Professor Zaehner's most sweeping statement regarding "the religion of Jesus Christ" as the consummation of other religions he asserts:

Christ indeed comes to fulfill not only the law and the prophets of Israel, but also the "law and the prophet" of the Āryan race. He fulfills or rounds out the conception of God independently revealed to the Hebrew prophets and to Zoroaster, and by His Crucifixion, Death, Resurrection, and Ascension He points to the type of mystical path the soul must tread if it is to rise beyond the *ātman* or higher self to its predestined reunion with God.[5]

It is precisely the attempt to find a hidden gospel in non-Christian religions or to see the religion of Jesus Christ as the fulfillment of other religions that jeopardizes Zaehner's contribution to interreligious understanding and dialogue. What is to keep the devoted Hindu theist from turning the tables and seeing the "religion of Krishna" as the fulfillment of the "religion of Jesus Christ"? or the Buddhist from seeing the Truth discovered by Siddhartha Gotama as the culmination of the insights taught by Christ? It seems likely that Professor Zaehner's approach, for all of its informed sympathy, leads to the juxtaposition and opposition of religious traditions.

Zaehner's methodology abets this problem. His description of a religion is almost exclusively in terms of its historical tradition. Its scriptures and doctrinal teachings seem to function as the exclusive authority on which analysis is based and by which judgments are made. For example, the description of the bond of love between man and God in the Hindu tradition is "as the text explicitly states." [6] When trying to understand a particular religion it is necessary to have an accurate knowledge of its scriptural and doctrinal background, but the question must be raised whether a religion is accurately represented merely in terms of its theological heritage. If the effort is one of historical description, then we have no quarrel with Professor Zaehner's approach. If, however, the attempt is to describe a living religion with which Christians are encouraged to enter into real dialogue, then this approach is found to be lacking.

One of the great virtues of the position of a scholar like Professor Zaehner is his emphasis on the place of the religious tradition. Yet, while valuable for a scholarly and historical understanding of a religious tradition, one wonders whether this approach does not present an unreal picture of a living religious faith. How many Hindus, Buddhists, or Christians understand their tradition with as much scholarly acumen as Professor Zaehner? Very few, in all probability. But, if interreligious understanding is to be real in terms of an open encounter and dialogue among religious persons, then the process must begin precisely with them. The religious tradition is the context in which faith arises and takes shape. It cannot, however, be taken as the absolute criterion descriptive of the faith of all the individuals within that tradition.

In contrast to the approach represented by R. C. Zaehner, Wilfred Cantwell Smith, professor of world religions and director of the Center for the Study of World Religions at Harvard University, insists that interreligious dialogue and understanding is fundamentally the concern of religious men; hence, expressions of personal faith should be considered prior to an analysis of historical traditions. Smith's focus on religious men gives his approach an existential flavor in much the same sense that Søren Kierkegaard is labeled an existentialist. Kierkegaard's existentialism was a humanistic affirmation of the centrality of the faith of the individual in relationship to God and a broadside attack on the Hegelian or any other system which stood in the way of that relationship. In a similar vein, Smith is critical of any approach to religious understanding that transmutes religion into a static system or that limits the religious life to its historic forms within a particular religious tradition. While Smith is keenly aware of religious traditions qua tradition, his attention is focused on the lives of religious men. Indeed, by his own admission, his approach may be typified as "personalistic."

Also analogous to Kierkegaard is Smith's understanding of the nature of *homo religiosus*. Both see religious man caught in the tension of the finite and the infinite, the mundane and the transmundane. In Smith's own words, the life of the religious man is suspended between the tension of "the mundane real of limiting and observable and changing reality and a realm transcending this." [7] Whatever the relationship between these two realms metaphysically or theologically, man himself is the link between the two.

From this assumption Professor Smith asserts that the study of man's religions in the past has been inadequate because it has focused either on the mundane or the transmundane and "has been confused in so far as its concept has attempted to embrace both." [8] In order to overcome this error Smith suggests that we dismiss the concept "religion" and employ the categories of "faith" and "tradition" (or "cumulative tradition"). By faith he means "an inner religious experience or involvement of a particular person; the impingement on him of the transcendent putative or real." [9] By tradition he intends the cumulative "mass of overt objective data that constitute the historical deposit . . . of the past religious life of the community in question." [10] With this distinction Professor Smith hopes, on the one hand, to avoid the pitfall of making religion a system of doctrines and practices and, on the other hand, to ensure that the student of religion will do justice to religions as historical phenomena (both collective and personal) while at the same time recognizing that they are not entirely limited by history.

From a rather shortsighted perspective, Smith's use of the two categories, faith and tradition, is simply a criticism of traditional ways of understanding religion. More profoundly, however, this criticism is based on an understanding of the life of the religious man suspended between the mundane and the transmundane. It is rooted, further-religion, or what might be more appropriately termed the pattern of man's religiousness.[11] Religion, fundamentally, is a way of life. The religious life is basic to the kind of relationship an individual has to himself, his fellowmen, and the ground of his existence. In Smith's view, the fundamental characteristic of the religious life is that it introduces the individual to that which is without limits.[12] In applying this proposition to Christianity one might say, the Christian life is a new life in a supernatural level.[13] Because the religious life is oriented to ultimate reality or, in other words, is lived on a supernatural level, religion is not to be taken simply as one aspect of a person's life. It is, rather, a total way of life, a comprehensive way of participating in or looking at all of life. From this perspective Smith describes a religious reformer as one who seeks not to reform a religion but to reform men's awareness of their total environment.[14]

Professor Smith's description of religion as a way of life in relationship to that which is without limits is not unlike Joachim Wach's characterization of religious experience as a total response of one's whole being to ultimate reality.[15] For both scholars the prior factor in religion is religious experience. From this religious "prior" stem various expressions or responses. Since for Smith religious experience is subsumed under the category of faith, he speaks of expressions of faith in art, community, "character," ritual and morality, ideas and words.[16] It is important to keep in mind that in Smith's approach, as in the approach of Joachim Wach, all aspects of the overt historical tradition are properly understood only in relationship to faith or religious experience. Thus, regarding religious statements Smith says, "The proper way to understand a religious statement is to endeavour . . . to see what they meant to the man who first uttered them, and what they have meant to those since for whom they have served as *expressions of their faith*." [17]

The essence of religion for Smith is the life of personal faith. A religious tradition functions as the context in which faith may arise. At its best, tradition is a channel of the religious life. At its worst, it obstructs religious vitality or serves as a substitute for faith.[18] Correspondingly, when one studies religion, the religious tradition at its best may reveal the true significance of the life of faith. At its worst, however, it may serve to obstruct "what the universe means to the religious man." [19]

Given the nature of religion, it becomes impossible to define either religion in general or a particular religion as an intelligible entity. A particular religion is not simply a historical tradition or the way in which the historical tradition has understood itself but a way of looking at the entire universe. For this reason a religion is difficult to conceptualize. On the one hand, it is a rich variety of factors comprehending all of life; on the other, every facet can be properly understood only in relationship to faith, that personal quality which characterizes the dialectic of the religious man resolved toward transcendence.

Professor Smith's approach to interreligious dialogue has a great appeal in its emphasis on religion as a way of life rather than as a static system. Interreligious dialogue becomes a revelatory experience, an experience of becoming and not merely of knowing or learning about. Thus, Smith states:

> I believe that there is a relation between a man's own personal faith and his understanding of the religious life of other men. I think that each is relevant to the other, and that it ought to be relevant. . . . Interreligious understanding is not merely an intellectual or academic or "objective" question. To ask about other men's faith is in itself to raise important issues about one's own.[20]

Smith's position, while appealing, is not without its problems. Whereas we can appreciate the thrust of his concern over the barrenness of the "ism" approach to the study of religion, his distinction between the categories of faith and tradition are somewhat arbitrary and may be misleading. There are many who would deny the possibility of making such a distinction. As Ninian Smart cogently remarks, it is surprising that even mystics whose experience of ultimate reality is inexpressible "go on to speak about religion in terms of the formulations of their own faith!"[21]

For Smith the ambiguity of the relationship between tradition and personal faith creates some difficult problems. In his Taylor lectures delivered at Yale Divinity School in 1963, Professor Smith makes the claim that the Christianity of one man may be "more true" than that of another, or again he says, "I also have two Muslim friends, of whom the religion of one is more true than the religion of the other."[22] But on what grounds can Smith make such a judgment? He has just said that religious truth lies only in persons ("The only question that concerns either God or me, or my neighbor is whether *my* Christianity is true, and whether *yours* is").[23] Given such an understanding of religious truth, by what criterion can he judge the religiousness of one man over another other than by his own private experience or by the testimony of the parties involved? Indeed, it would even seem presumptuous to set for oneself the task of making such a judgment.

A similar problem emerges when Professor Smith states that the terms "true" and "false" do not refer to some sort of prototype of a particular religious tradition but "to the prototype of what religion ought to be." [24] From Smith's personalistic stance, does the prototype of what religion ought to be not run the danger of being what *I* think religion ought to be? If so, then Smith's approach to interreligious dialogue would tend to pit one person's religious experience against another's just as R. C. Zaehner's approach would seem to juxtapose religious traditions.

No one approach to open and mutual interreligious dialogue and understanding is perfect, but in our opinion the position of Wilfred Cantwell Smith offers the most fruitful possibility of genuine and significant encounter. For instance, Smith's approach has the preeminent virtue of allowing us to engage the position of someone like Bhikkhu Buddhadāsa as it is (see Chapter IV). We need not try to justify it in terms of some abstraction of orthodox Theravāda doctrine, nor do we need to excuse Buddhadāsa's "eccentricities" on the grounds of influence from Mahāyāna (as some have done). Either of these attempts would greatly devalue the genuine significance of Buddhadāsa's thought for Thai Buddhism as well as his contribution to interreligious dialogue in Thailand.

The position of Buddhadāsa, as well as of other informed Buddhists with whom we have spoken, also supports Smith's observation that Buddhism and in particular early Buddhism is a "joyous proclamation of a discovery of a truth without which life is bleak." [25] Furthermore, states Smith, the Buddha's teaching of infinite compassion is based on this truth and must be taken seriously.[26] By way of contrast, it is interesting to note R. C. Zaehner's *"amazement"* that the Buddha, "the preacher of a complete detachment from all worldly things," could in the same breath speak of "compassion" and "selfless giving." [27] Zaehner is here reflecting the penchant of Western scholars to see Theravāda Buddhism as basically pessimistic, a misunderstanding based on certain scholarly analyses that might have been overcome had there been more of a real encounter among religious persons.

Bhikkhu Buddhadāsa's emphasis on the centrality of Dhamma and his understanding of it vis à vis the God concept in Christianity lends additional support to Smith's approach. Smith says, "I have the feeling that for most Buddhists the dominant and central concept is Dharma" and that is "akin to the notion of God in the West." [28] Although Professor Smith's emphasis on Dhamma as moral law is not so strong in Buddhadāsa's thought, the latter clearly would agree that Dhamma is an "absolute reality immediately available to every man." [29]

We are not trying to prove that the content of the positions of W. C. Smith and Bhikkhu Buddhadāsa is identical. Rather, we are suggesting that Smith's approach to religious situations allows interreligious dialogue to take place on the level of persons rather than systems. We believe that this approach has the virtue of more accurately representing religions as they are. Furthermore, it would appear that on this level, the level of honest and open encounter, there are probably more similarities between a "theist" like Dr. Smith and an "atheist" like Bhikkhu Buddhadāsa than an analysis of doctrines or texts might have indicated.

TAKING BUDDHISM SERIOUSLY

In the preceding section we endeavored to point to an approach to Buddhism characterized by an open acceptance of religious persons. We must now move beyond the question of attitude and understanding to the question of the impact of Buddhism on Western religious thought and practice. It is not a new question but today it holds new promise because of both an increasing awareness of Buddhist Asia in the West and a growing receptivity to new values and ideals. It would be a gross distortion to claim that Buddhism has made a significant impact on the life and thought of the Judeo-Christian tradition in America. Its greatest appeal has been among such subcultural groups as the beats and the hippies, although a serious academic interest in Buddhism and other Asian religions is flourishing on many college campuses. A few churchmen, especially in the Roman Catholic tradition, are also beginning to take Asian religions seriously. Probably the best known has been Thomas Merton, whose writings on mysticism are widely read by Catholics and Protestants alike. In recent years Merton turned with increasing interest to a study of Taoism and Buddhism especially.[30] In fact, his untimely death in 1968 occurred while he was on a trip to Asia studying Asian religions at first hand.

In particular, Father Merton was attracted to Zen Buddhism. He sees Zen making an important contribution to modern man's liberation from inordinate self-conscious-

ness. In contrast to the Western religious traditions' preoccupation with *explanation*, Zen plunges men back to a
ground of direct *experience*: "Zen is not Kerygma, but
realization, not revelation but consciousness. . . ." [31] Merton believes this emphasis in Zen offers a means of cutting
through the Christian's inevitable tendency to lose the
personal, experiential dimension of religion and life. It is
not that Christianity lacks the experiential dimension;
rather, it has simply been overshadowed by an undue
emphasis on exposition and explanation.

In the manner of a man who prizes the firsthand quality
of the religious life, Father Merton contends that at heart
both Christianity and Buddhism aim at ontological transformation through direct experience. The Word of the
Cross demands a radical transformation of consciousness,
not a discourse by the rational intellect! The experience
of dying and rising with Christ is likened by Merton to
the Zen notion of the "Great Death" experience associated
with *satori*, or enlightenment. In brief, Father Merton is
claiming that Christians as well as Buddhists must practice
Zen if their religion is to be vital, dynamic, and ontologi-
cally significant. Zen is that form of religion par excellence
which plunges men toward "the quest for direct and pure
experience on a metaphysical level liberated from verbal
formulas and linguistic preconceptions." [32]

Father Merton sees many parallels between Christianity
and Zen. He follows D. T. Suzuki in finding similarities
between Meister Eckhart and the Zen Masters to the
point that "whatever Zen may be . . . it is somehow in
Eckhart." [33] Merton also discovers in Christianity and in
Zen the tendency to *transform* ordinary, everyday human
existence rather than reject it and sees parallels between
such concepts as the Zen notion of Emptiness or Non-

action (*wu wei*) and the New Testament concept of the freedom of the sons of God: "Not that they are theologically one and the same, but they have at any rate the same kind of limitlessness, the same kind of inhibition, the same psychic fullness of creativity which mark the fully integrated maturity of the 'enlightened self.' " [34] What Father Merton seems to be saying is that the reality to which Paul attests when he speaks of no longer seeing through a glass darkly but face to face (I Cor., ch. 13) is an experience in which both Christianity and Zen demand a radical transformation of being, a growth from childhood to mature manhood, indeed, a new creation. It is especially interesting that in his later writings, such as *Zen and the Birds of Appetite*, Father Merton perceives the same quality of religious experience in both Zen and Christianity. As a Christian he can speak of a Zen-like attitude toward life which could serve to rejuvenate that mode of religious experience shared by both Christianity and Buddhism.

Another contemporary American Catholic attracted by Buddhism is Dom Aelred Graham, former prior of the Benedictine community in Portsmouth, Rhode Island. Although Graham is more tightly bound by Thomistic categories than is Thomas Merton, he makes some interesting suggestions regarding ways in which Zen Buddhism could benefit Christianity. Thus he points out that the emphasis on harmony and naturalness in Zen can serve to bring out the Thomistic concept of the conaturalness of God and man as a means of overcoming modern man's sense of alienation from his fellowman and his natural environment. Among his other suggestions is an appreciation for the Buddhist recognition of the universality of egocentricity and the consequent need of nonattachment as the only means by which one can both enjoy an experience and yet not be involved in it.[35] Unlike the mystic, Father Merton, Dom Aelred Graham's Christian theism is always worn on his sleeve, so to speak. Yet, Zen is able to make a contribution even at this point: "Placed in the context of faith in God and our dependence on His grace, the Zen insight may cleanse the Christian mind a little . . . from an overburdening sense of guilt . . . , from anxiety and remorse. . . . The mind being so clarified, God's presence, adjusted to Ultimate Reality, is 'realized' —now where I am." [36]

Among Protestants, appreciation of Asian religions appears to be more limited. Thomas J. J. Altizer, one of the so-called "death of God" theologians, is one who is interested in Buddhism, and critics of Altizer claim that his immanentist theology shows evidences of influences from the East.[37] It is Alan Watts who has taken Asian religions, especially Zen Buddhism, most to heart, however. Watts is not exactly the theologian's theologian. Indeed, when the author was in seminary not so many years ago Watts was not even mentioned. Among college students, however, he is widely read. In a series of four theological works[38] he describes a position "beyond theology" that is basically unitary and relational (panentheistic) and, hence, closer to the Hindu Ātman-Brahman or the Buddhist Dharmakāya than to a model of theological monarchism. It is a mystical religion, a religion of the spirit that deplores distinctions and definitions as fundamentally inimical to a Ground-of-Being God beyond both sensible and conceptual images. Watts contends that the religions of Asia are based on such a unifying world view which offers a release from conflict and anxiety, a state of being in which oppositions become mutually cooperative in-

stead of mutually exclusive.[39] Christianity, in Watts's
opinion, has represented an opposing world view, one
based on absolute distinctions between good and evil,
life and death. This perspective results in an inevitable
drive toward self-justification, a flurry of do-good activism
rather than a life-style based on the realization that all
polarities are relative and mutually interdependent.

Watts's position is a naturalistic, "letting-go," "this-is-
it" type of faith based on the conviction that Christianity's
conception of God is too small because the Christian's
traditional view of man has been too limited:

> To construct a God in the human image is objection-
> able only to the extent that we have a poor image of
> ourselves . . . . But as we can begin to visualize man
> as the behavior of a unified field— immensely com-
> plex and comprising the whole universe— there is
> less and less reason against conceiving God in *that*
> image. To go deeper and deeper into oneself is also
> to go farther and farther out into the universe, until
> . . . we reach the domain where three-dimensional,
> sensory images are no longer valid.[40]

Such a cosmic awareness or consciousness involves the
"abandonment of proprietorship" of both the external
world of nature and the internal world of the human
organization, thereby freeing the individual to live in
genuine oneness with all things.[41]

Watts's religion of experience and feeling shares Merton's view that Zen restores the primacy of life directly
lived as well as a theological reality essentially beyond
definition. Unlike Merton, however, Watts oversimplifies
both Christianity and the religions of Asia. As Merton's
writings well illustrate, it is unfair to stereotype Christianity in terms of a monarchical theism or ethical dualism

and it is a very inadequate generalization of Hinduism and Buddhism to say that when it comes to the great conflicts of feeling and action their answer is close to an "anything goes" attitude of instinctual romanticism.[42] Although Watts often contends that he represents an Asian religion viewpoint, he is overly simplistic and sometimes misrepresents Hinduism and Buddhism; nevertheless, he should be taken more seriously as one of the few contemporary theologians who has explicitly attempted to incorporate the insights of Buddhism into his own position. Alan Watts will never be a theologian's theologian. A seminary will probably never offer a seminar on his writings. But, he will continue to influence college students and his cathartic position should be more deeply appreciated—much as the provocative humor of a Zen anecdote.

Our main task in this section is not to describe the positions of theologians who have been influenced by Buddhism but to develop some preliminary suggestions of the way in which Buddhism might provoke religious reflection and theological renewal. In the past, Buddhism has been either cloaked with the mystique of the Orient or preempted by cultural fringe groups. It is time Christian theologians took Buddhism more seriously. As an illustration of the way in which this might be done, three cardinal ideas in Theravāda Buddhism will be applied to Christianity: impermanence (*anicca*), detachment (*upekkhā*), and no-self (*anatta*). Our explication aims not at synthesis but at stimulation and provocation.

As pointed out in Chapter I, Theravāda Buddhism rests on a view of the world as ever-changing or noneternal (*anicca*). The ethical consequence of this view is to inculcate a healthy skepticism toward excessive involve-

ment in mundane affairs. Attachment to the world produces suffering because attachment assumes a permanence
not really there. Some critics of Buddhism claim that this
teaching nullifies the possibility of a positive and con-
structive ethic typical of the Western religious tradition.
Historically such a charge breaks down, although the
teaching of *anicca* has undoubtedly affected the distinction between ultimate (Nibbāna) and proximate (*kamma-
saṁsāra*) goals and between monastic and lay life. One of
the great virtues of the teaching that change is a normative fact of life is the contextual perspective it provides for
every human endeavor. The validity of human action is
not undermined, but its *ultimate* value is thrown into
question.

The doctrine of *anicca* is not without its counterpart
in the Judeo-Christian tradition. Think for a moment of
such New Testament passages as: "Do not lay up for
yourselves treasures on earth, where moth and rust consume and where thieves break in and steal, but lay up for
yourselves treasures in heaven, where neither moth nor
rust consumes and where thieves do not break in and
steal. For where your treasure is, there will your heart be
also" (Matt. 6:19–21). The New Testament, of course,
presumes a very different set of theological assumptions
than does Theravāda Buddhism. Yet, both are suspicious
of a way of life dedicated to the pursuit of mundane ends.
Both recognize the limited satisfactions of such goals and
point beyond them to other and more lasting ones.

Both Theravāda Buddhism and the New Testament
accept the world for what it is even though their analyses
vary. Neither rejects the world, but both reject its adamant
claims for ultimate loyalty. This rejection is illustrated
in the two traditions in the mythical or legendary aspects

of the biography of each tradition's founder. Significantly enough, when each receives the authority of charismatic office he is tested by the power of the sensory or mundane world. In the New Testament this power of evil is personified by Satan in the form of a tempter (Matt. 4:1–11), and in the Pāli scripture a parallel device is used. Before the Buddha's enlightenment he is tempted by Mara and the forces of evil to give his allegiance to them (Jātaka 1:71 ff.). As we know, both the Christ and the Buddha assume heroic proportions in their victory over the temptations put in their way.

In the New Testament tradition the tentativeness that characterizes man's relationship to the world is closely associated with the eschatological hope. Jesus as the new Messiah ushers in a New Aeon, but it is yet unfulfilled. The command is to repent, to prepare for the coming of the Kingdom of God. Christians are expected to live a life distinctive from the rest of the world in expectation of the Second Coming of the Christ, as so many of Paul's admonitions declare. The Christian church, in the New Testament view, is the community of the not-yet-fully-saved.

This dimension of the Christian tradition, so central to the New Testament faith, is easily lost within the matrix of cultural Christianity. The church, rather than a community of people living in expectation of the fulfillment of a future hope, inevitably becomes part of an establishment already arrived. Rather than a healthy skepticism toward the mundane world, it wholly embraces the world as the arena in which God acts out his drama of salvation. All too often the theological significance of this claim is transposed into cultural terms, and the goals of the religion become largely synonymous with the goals of the society.

Buddhism encounters Christianity at this point with a twofold result. On the one hand, it calls on the Christian to adopt a critical stance toward the claims of the world from his own ethical and eschatological perspective. On the other, Buddhism brings its own interpretation of the world as a realm of continual change and even more radically than the Christian tradition orders men not to lay up treasures on earth. Perhaps the Buddhist analysis of the world has something to offer the Christian at this particular moment in history. As acknowledged at the beginning of this study, we are living in an age of rapid change. At the same time, the advantages of a highly developed technological society provoke the illusion of providing for all the wants of man. The Buddhist critique offers a corrective to this illusion and throws out the reminder that men in all ages live on the cutting edge of change. This reminder need not lead to despair. On the contrary, as Alan Watts points out, to accept the inevitability of change and insecurity leads to a more realistic and happier life-style.[43]

A second cardinal teaching of Theravāda Buddhism is the concept of *upekkhā*, or detachment. The term occurs in several contexts in the Pāli scriptures, but perhaps the most important is as the fourth and final stage of mental development, known as the Divine Abodes (*brahma vihāra*) or states of unlimited consciousness (*appamañña*). In classical Theravāda texts such as Buddhaghosa's Path of Purity (Visuddhimagga), *upekkhā* is a state of mind reached through the discipline of meditation and is, if you will, a detachment or equanimity attained through a total program of spiritual training.

There are two aspects of the Buddhist teaching associated with *upekkhā* especially relevant to Christianity. The first is fundamentally theological and the other more practical or programmatic. Theologically the Christian faith centers on the incarnation, the Christ event, the paradox of the divine entering history in the person of Jesus, the Christ. There are two sides to the incarnation— the divine and the human, but in popular Christian thought the human side predominates. At Christmas, Christians delight in stories of the infant Jesus, and in the season of Lent agonize in the passion of the man crucified on the cross. Theologians and ministers appeal to an incarnational theology to justify commitment to the work of the church or involvement in various social service projects. It is as though involvement for involvement's sake is a Christian virtue because that is what the incarnation represents in terms of the life of an individual or the church. Such a stance is an unfortunate caricature of an incarnational theology, since it neglects the divine side of the Christ event. As the Prologue to the Gospel of John makes so clear, the incarnation, the Word made flesh, is to be understood in the perspective of the Word, which from the beginning has been involved in the creative process. The incarnation is not simply a moment of historical time signified by the Christ event; it is the Word of the beginning designated by a historical event which through faith becomes an eternal Now. In this event is implied not simply involvement in the historical but the detachment of the eternal. Here is not only the passion of human suffering but the joy of divine giving.

Buddhism reminds Christians of the objective, detached side of faith. Christian faith is not blind but a faith seeking understanding. It embraces an objective and critical stance toward all human institutions and activities, even those of the church itself. Faith is openness toward every possibility because there are no grounds for defensiveness about any of its own systems or structures. Faith is laughing at the seriousness of life for the paradoxical reason that God chose to die on a cross. The *upekkhā* aspect of faith is one very much needed in today's world of explosive tensions.

The more practical or programmatic application of Buddhist detachment arises from the context in which *upekkhā* is generally discussed in the Theravāda texts, namely, meditation. Christianity, in contrast to Buddhism, has been singularly lacking in forms of religious discipline. There are good theological and historical reasons for this fact. However, it has left the church, especially the Protestant Church, to flounder at a time when its sociological function is being assumed by secular organizations and its worship function called into question by the theological revolution. Might it not be that the church could learn from the religious disciplines of Buddhist meditation? We are not necessarily suggesting that the corner church institute classes in meditation, although there might be ways in which this could be done. Is there any reason, for example, why the growing use of sensitivity training groups in churches could not be modified by the Buddhist use of disciplined concentration and self-understanding? The methods are clearly different. Yet, if the practice of awareness (*sati*) is successful, it not only leads to a more profound self-understanding but enhances one's total awareness of life and develops the powers of objective analysis and understanding. Furthermore, if the theological side of detachment (*uppekhā*) is at all valid, the practice of meditative awareness and concentration offers a practical means to realize a theological truth. We have noted that in the past the practice of meditation among

Buddhists was reserved for the monks but that in the modern period it is developing an appeal among laymen. Perhaps the time has also arrived in the West for religious disciplines, once the special prerogative of the cloister, to become a part of the lay world.

The third Buddhist teaching to be applied to Christianity is the concept of no-self (*anatta*). It has already been pointed out that some psychologists have grown suspicious of the Freudian ego (see Chapter III). From the perspective of Christianity there is a degree of similarity between the Christian notion of selflessness and the Buddhist doctrine of no-self. Winston King points to two similarities: Both see self-love as destructive of larger spiritual possibilities, and for both traditions the "saint . . . is so unified with himself, so purified . . . that he instinctively responds to every situation that confronts him in a fully Christian or Buddhist manner." [44]

One might say that Buddhism has nothing to add to Christianity at this point, yet the vehement insistence of the Buddhist cannot help causing the Christian to pause and rethink the significance of selflessness. What does it mean for a man to "deny himself and take up his cross and follow me"? Ethically, Christianity has interpreted this commandment in terms of selfless service. The text from which the above quotation is taken, however, offers the possibility of an interpretation that goes beyond this concept: "Whoever would save his life would lose it, and whoever loses his life for my sake will find it" (Matt. 16:25). In Pauline terms, Christian selflessness means dying to the Old Self and being reborn to the New. It is to become the new creation in which "it is no longer I who live, but Christ who lives in me" (Gal. 2:20). The vocabulary of mysticism might label this claim of Paul's "deification," but it would be more descriptive of Pauline thought to say that to have Christ living in me means to have emptied myself by faith in order to be filled by the power of the Spirit. The Christian loss of Self is always coupled with the gaining of a New Self; one dies in order to receive new life, or gives oneself up in faith in order to receive the life-giving power of the Holy Spirit. The main function of Buddhism in regard to a Christian view of man is to act as a *provocateur*, to recall the centrality of the Christian theme of death and rebirth, of new being.

We have attempted to point to a few ways in which Buddhism might influence Christian thought today. Although it is not out of the question that Buddhism in the West will become increasingly important in its own right, its greatest contribution will probably be measured by the degree to which it challenges and perhaps modifies ideas and practices within the Western religious traditions. At the present time Buddhism in Southeast Asia is facing a serious test as the cultural societies of which it is a part move toward modernity. In confronting this challenge, it is questionable whether Buddhism will be able to maintain its viability. Yet, the same might be said of the religious traditions of the West. Will they be able to survive the forces of social and technological change? The prospects of both traditions will be brighter if each benefits from the spiritual insights and wisdom of the other.

NOTES

INTRODUCTION

1. For a discussion of developments in Chinese Buddhism in the twentieth century, see Holmes Welch, *The Revival of Buddhism in China* (Harvard University Press, 1968).

2. Robert N. Bellah, "Epilogue: Religion and Progress in Modern Asia," in *Religion and Progress in Modern Asia*, ed. by Robert N. Bellah (The Free Press, 1965), p. 172.

3. See Charles Y. Glock and Rodney Stark, *Religion and Society in Tension* (Rand McNally & Company, 1965).

4. H. Richard Niebuhr, *Christ and Culture* (Harper & Brothers, 1951). It should be noted that citing these categories here slightly alters Niebuhr's focal problem— "the double wrestle of the church with its Lord and with the cultural society with which it lives in symbiosis."

5. *Ibid.*, p. 83.

6. Bellah, "Epilogue: Religion and Progress in Modern Asia," in Bellah (ed.), *Religion and Progress* . . . , p. 193.

7. *Ibid.*, p. 194.

8. *Ibid.*, p. 174.

9. Soedjatmoko, "Cultural Motivations to Progress: The 'Exterior' and the 'Interior' Views," in Bellah (ed.), *Religion and Progress* . . . , p. 7.

10. *Ibid.*, p. 8.

CHAPTER I. BUDDHISM AND ASIA

1. Bellah, "Epilogue: Religion and Progress in Modern Asia," *Religion and Progress* . . . , p. 203.

2. "Theravāda" means the teachings (*vāda*) of the elders (*thera*) and refers to the form of Buddhism that centered in Ceylon and gradually became the orthodox religion in much of Southeast Asia. It is sometimes referred to as Southern Buddhism and bears the canonical language of Pāli. (Citations of Buddhist terms will be given in Pāli.) By way of contrast, the forms of Buddhism that became predominant in China, Korea, and Japan are referred to as Mahāyāna ("Great Vehicle"), or Northern Buddhism, with the earliest Indian texts being in Sanskrit. A third type of Buddhism is known as the Tantrayāna or Vajrayāna ("Thunderbolt Vehicle"), which came to be the state religion in Tibet and is found throughout Central and East Asia.

3. Joseph Campbell, *The Hero with a Thousand Faces* (Meridian Books, The World Publishing Company, 1956), pp. 30 ff.

4. See Sukumar Dutt, *Early Buddhist Monachism*, rev. ed. (Bombay: Asia Publishing House, 1960), Ch. II.

5. *Woven Cadences* (Sutta Nipāta), tr. by E. M. Hare, quoted in Bhikkhu Khantipālo, "With Robes and Bowl," *The Wheel*, No. 83/84 (Kandy: Buddhist Publication Society, 1965), p. 3.

6. Aśoka, *Edicts of Aśoka*, tr. and ed. by N. A. Nikam and R. McKeon (The University of Chicago Press, 1959), p. 43.

7. *Buddhism in Translations*, ed. and tr. by Henry C. Warren (Atheneum Publishers, 1963), p. 129.

8. *Ibid.*, p. 131.

9. The twelve stages of the Dependent Origination series are described in a number of texts and commentaries. See Nyanatiloka Mahathera, "The Significance of Dependent Origination in Theravada Buddhism," *The Wheel*, No. 140 (1969).

10. Edward Conze, *Buddhist Thought in India* (London: George Allen & Unwin, Ltd., 1962), p. 57.

11. Many of the traditional doctrines of Buddhism occur

as formulas, partly for mnemonic reasons. Not only were these teachings passed on orally for generations, but even today monks memorize many Pāli chants. The Four Noble Truths, frequently referred to as the essence of classical Theravāda doctrine, teach that the nature of existence is suffering (*dukkha*), the cause of its arising (*samudaya*) is desire or thirst (*tanha*), the cessation (*nirodha*) of desire brings the cessation of suffering, and a special path (*magga*) is to be followed for the cessation of suffering.

CHAPTER II. BUDDHISM AND NATIONALISM

1. Richard A. Gard, *Buddhism* (Washington Square Press, Inc., 1963), p. 203.

2. Joseph M. Kitagawa, "Buddhism and Asian Politics," *Asian Survey*, Vol. II, No. 5 (July, 1962), p. 4.

3. Fred von der Mehden, "Buddhism and Politics in Burma," *Antioch Review*, Vol. XXI, No. 2 (Summer, 1961), p. 168.

4. Kitagawa, *Asian Survey*, Vol. II, No. 5, p. 7.

5. *Ibid.*

6. See Gard, *Buddhism*, pp. 202–214. Also, Richard A. Gard, "Buddhism and Political Authority," in *The Ethic of Power*, ed. by Harold D. Lasswell and Harlan Cleveland (Harper & Row, Publishers, Inc., 1962), pp. 43–48.

7. The term "Sāsana" refers to the teaching of the Buddha, and hence comes to mean the religion of the followers of those teachings (i.e., Buddhism).

8. Robert Heine-Geldern, *Conceptions of State and Kingship in Southeast Asia* (Southeast Asia Program Data Papers, No. 18; Cornell University Department of Asian Studies, 1956), p. 9.

9. The following are some of the many studies relevant to Buddhism and politics in Burma: Hting Aung, "Commentary," in *Nationalism and Progress in Free Asia*, ed. by Philip W. Thayer (Johns Hopkins Press, 1963), pp. 82–95; Heinz Bechert, *Buddhismus, Staat und Gesellschaft in den Ländern des Theravada-Buddhismus*, Vol. II (Wiesbaden: Otto Harfassowitz, 1967), Chs. 34 to 37; Richard Butwell, "Four Failures of U Nu's Second Premiership," *Asian Survey*, Vol. II,

No. 3 (March, 1963), pp. 3–11; Winston L. King, "Buddhism and Political Power in Burma," in *Studies on Asia,* Vol. III, ed. by Sidney Brown (University of Nebraska Press, 1962), pp. 9–19; Von der Mehden, "Buddhism and Politics in Burma," pp. 166–175; Fred von der Mehden, *Religion and Nationalism in Southeast Asia* (University of Wisconsin Press, 1963); E. Sarkisyanz, *Buddhist Backgrounds of the Burmese Revolution* (The Hague: Martinus Nijhoff, 1965); E. Sarkisyanz, "On the Place of U Nu's Buddhist Socialism in Burma's History of Ideas," in *Studies on Asia,* Vol. II, ed. by Robert K. Sakai (University of Nebraska Press, 1961); Donald E. Smith, *Religion and Politics in Burma* (Princeton University Press, 1965).

10. John F. Cady, *A History of Modern Burma* (Cornell University Press, 1958), p. 190.

11. Government of the Union of Burma Land Nationalization Act, 1948, p. 29, para. 29, quoted in Sarkisyanz, *Buddhist Backgrounds of the Burmese Revolution,* p. 215.

12. *Ibid.*

13. Richard Butwell, *U Nu of Burma* (Stanford University Press, 1963), p. 65.

14. *The Nation,* Oct. 26, 1958, quoted in Butwell, *U Nu of Burma,* p. 62.

15. Donald E. Smith, *Religion and Politics in Burma,* pp. 318–319.

16. For information on Buddhism and politics in Ceylon, see: Michael Ames, "Religion, Politics and Economic Development in Ceylon: An Interpretation of the Weber Thesis," in *Proceedings of the 1964 Annual Spring Meeting of the American Ethnological Society,* ed. by M. E. Spiro (University of Washington Press, 1969), pp. 61–76; Heinz Bechert, *Buddhismus, Staat und Gesellschaft in den Ländern des Theravada-Buddhismus,* Vol. I (Berlin: Alfred Metzner, 1966), Ch. 29; B. H. Farmer, "The Social Basis of Nationalism in Ceylon," *Journal of Asian Studies,* Vol. XXIV, No. 3 (May, 1965), pp. 431–439; G. Obeyesekere, "Religious Symbolism and Political Change in Ceylon" (Paper read at the Burg Wartensten Symposium on Local-Level Politics, July 5–14, 1966; offset copy); Marshall R. Singer, *The Emerging Elite: A Study of Political Leadership in Ceylon* (MIT

Press, 1964); A. Jeyaratnam Wilson, "Buddhism in Ceylon Politics," in *South Asian Politics and Religion*, ed. by Donald E. Smith (Princeton University Press, 1966), Ch. 23; W. Howard Wriggins, *Ceylon: Dilemmas of a New Nation* (Princeton University Press, 1960), Ch. 6.

17. Farmer, *Journal of Asian Studies*, Vol. XXIV, No. 3, p. 433.

18. Donald E. Smith, "The Sinhalese Buddhist Revolution," in Smith (ed.), *South Asian Politics and Religion*, p. 456.

19. S.W.R.D. Bandaranaike, *Speeches and Writings* (Colombo: Department of Broadcasting and Information, 1963), p. 308.

20. Jerrold Schechter, *The New Face of Buddha* (Tokyo: John Weatherill, Inc., 1967), p. 68.

21. *Ibid.*, p. 69.

22. For additional material on Buddhism and politics in Vietnam, see: Bechert, *Buddhismus, Staat und Gesellschaft* . . . , Vol. II, Ch. 50; Paul van Cain, "Buddhism and Politics in Vietnam," *Christianity and Crisis*, Vol. XXVI, No. 12 (July 11, 1966), pp. 156–159; Thich Nhat Hanh, *Vietnam, Lotus in a Sea of Fire* (London: SCM Press, Ltd., 1967); Charles Joiner, "South Vietnam's Buddhist Crisis: Organization for Clarity, Dissidence and Unity," *Asian Survey*, Vol. IV, No. 7 (July, 1964), pp. 915–929; Jack Langguth, "The Buddhist Way in Vietnam," *The New York Times Magazine*, Oct. 11, 1966, pp. 29 ff.; Schechter, *The New Face of Buddha*, Chs. 9 to 11.

23. Van Cain, *Christianity and Crisis*, Vol. XXVI, No. 12, pp. 156–159. See also Hanh, *Vietnam, Lotus in a Sea of Fire*, pp. 50 f.

24. Joiner, *Asian Survey*, Vol. IV, No. 7, p. 925.

25. *Ibid.*, p. 927.

26. Schechter, *The New Face of Buddha*, p. 206.

27. *Ibid.*

28. See Hanh, *Vietnam, Lotus in a Sea of Fire*, Ch. III.

29. *The Ceylon Daily News*, Nov. 5, 1965.

30. Memorandum and Articles of the Ceylon Farmers' Association, 1966, p. 1. Italics mine.

31. "Poya" is an abbreviation of the Pāli word *uposatha*,

the Buddhist Sabbath Day calculated according to the four phases of the moon.

32. *The Betrayal of Buddhism*, An Abridged Version of the Report of the Buddhist Committee of Inquiry (Balangoda: Dharmavijaya Press, 1956), Foreword.

33. *Ibid.*, p. 124.

34. *Ibid.*, p. 101.

35. *Ibid.*, p. 105.

36. G. C. Mendis, *Ceylon Today and Yesterday* (Colombo: Associated Newspapers of Ceylon, Ltd., 1957), pp. 110–111.

37. Soka Gakkai is one of the so-called new religions in Japan. These religions form an interesting subject of study in and of themselves but fall outside the focus of our attention. For further reference to the new religions and Soka Gakkai in particular, see: James A. Dator, "The Soka-Gakkai: A Socio-Political Interpretation," *Contemporary Religions in Japan*, Vol. VI (September, 1965), pp. 205–242, James A. Dator, *Soka Gakkai, Builders of the Third Civilization* (University of Washington Press, 1969); Daisaku Ikeda, *Complete Works of Daisaku Ikeda*, Vol. I (Tokyo: The Seikyo Press, 1968); H. Neill McFarland, *The Rush Hour of the Gods: A Study of New Religious Movements in Japan* (The Macmillan Company, 1967), Ch. 9; Felix Moos, "Religion and Politics in Japan; The Case of Soka Gakkai," *Asian Survey*, Vol. III, No. 3 (March, 1963), pp. 136–142; Robert Ramseyer, "The Soka Gakkai and the Japanese Local Elections of 1960," *Contemporary Religions in Japan*, Vol. IV (December, 1963), pp. 287–304; Henry Thomsen, *The New Religions of Japan* (Charles E. Tuttle Company, Inc., 1963).

38. Dator, *Soka Gakkai, Builders of the Third Civilization*, p. 12.

39. Moos, *Asian Survey*, Vol. III, No. 3, p. 141.

40. Dator, *Soka Gakkai, Builders of the Third Civilization*, p. 5.

41. Ikeda, *Complete Works* . . . , pp. 211–213.

CHAPTER III. BUDDHISM AND "CULTURAL REVOLUTION"

1. For information on Buddhist social ethics, see: K. N. Jayatilleke, "Aspects of Buddhist Social Philosophy," *The Wheel*, No. 128/129 (1969); K. N. Jayatilleke, *The Princi-*

ples of International Law in Buddhist Doctrine (Leiden: A. W. Sijthoff, 1968); Winston L. King, *In the Hope of Nibbāna: An Essay on Theravāda Buddhist Ethics* (The Open Court Publishing Company, 1964), Chs. 7 to 9; Winston L. King, "New Forces in an Old Culture," *Antioch Review,* Vol. XXI, No. 2 (Summer, 1961), pp. 155–164; G. P. Malalasakera and K. N. Jayatilleke, *Buddhism and the Race Question* (Paris: UNESCO, 1958); Elizabeth Nottingham, "Buddhist Ethics and Economic Development," *World Buddhism Vesak Annual* (Dehiwela: Buddhist Publication, 1967), pp. 37–39; Walpola Rahula, *What the Buddha Taught* (Bedford, England: Gordon Fraser Gallery, Ltd., 1959), Ch. 7; D. C. Wijewardene, *The Revolt in the Temple* (Colombo: Sinha Publications, 1953), Part III.

2. Donald E. Smith, "The Political Monks and Monastic Reform," in Smith (ed.), *South Asian Politics and Religion,* p. 509.

3. Wijewardene, *The Revolt in the Temple,* p. 586.

4. See Jayatilleke, *The Wheel,* No. 128/129, pp. 1–24.

5. Ikeda, *Complete Works . . . ,* p. 261.

6. Pin Mutugan, *Kaa Panhaa Chow Baan* (Bangkok: Khlang Withaja, 1957), p. 58.

7. *Ibid.,* p. 62. Translation mine.

8. *Ibid.,* p. 68.

9. Bhikkhu Paññānanda, *Chumnum Ryang San* (Bangkok: Khlang Withaja, 1955), p. 145. Translation mine.

10. *Ibid.,* p. 141.

11. Rahula, *What the Buddha Taught,* p. 88.

12. For information on Buddhist education, see: Bechert, *Buddhismus, Staat und Gesellschaft . . . ,* Vol. I, Part III; Ernst Benz, *Buddhism or Communism: Which Holds the Future of Asia?* (London: George Allen & Unwin, Ltd., 1966), Ch. V; G. P. Malalasekera, "Fundamental Ideals of Buddhist Education," *The Buddhist Vesak Annual* (Colombo: Y.M.B.A., 1967), pp. 253–256; Phra Mahā Prayuddha, "Sangha in Modern Society," *Visakha Puja* (Bangkok: Buddhist Association of Thailand, 1968), pp. 58–73; Robert H. Lawson Slater, "Modern Trends in Theravāda Buddhism," in *Modern Trends in World Religions,* ed. by Joseph M. Kitagawa (The Open Court Publishing Company, 1959), pp. 223–225.

13. Mendis, *Ceylon Today and Yesterday*, p. 153.

14. *The Buddhist*, Vol. XXXVII, No. 3 (August, 1966), p. 90.

15. *Ibid.*

16. *The Buddhist*, Vol. XXXVIII, No. 2 (July, 1967), p. 47.

17. *The Buddhist*, Vol. XXXVII, No. 1 (June, 1966), p. 7.

18. See Prayuddha, "Sangha in Modern Society," pp. 58–73.

19. L. G. Hewage, "Some Aspects of Buddhist Higher Education," *The Ceylon Daily News*, Oct. 9, 1967.

20. For information on Buddhism and science, see: Benz, *Buddhism or Communism . . . ?* Ch. V; Douglas M. Burns, "Buddhist Meditation and Depth Psychology," *The Wheel*, No. 88/89 (1966); U Chan Htoon, "Buddhism and the Age of Science," *The Wheel*, No. 36/37 (1967); Ikeda, *Complete Works . . .* , Vol. I, Part II; Akira Kasamatsu and Tomio Hirai, "Science of Zazen," *Psychologia*, Vol. V, No. 4 (December, 1962), pp. 86–91; Winston L. King, *A Thousand Lives Away* (Harvard University Press, 1964), Ch. IV; P. Ranasingha, *Buddha's Explanation of the Universe* (Colombo: Ministry of Education, 1958); Francis Story, "The Case for Rebirth," *The Wheel*, No. 12/13 (1964); Luang Suriyabongs, *Buddhism in the Light of Modern Scientific Ideas*, rev. ed. (Bangkok: Mahamakut Academy, 1960); D. T. Suzuki, Erich Fromm, Richard DeMartino, *Zen Buddhism and Psychoanalysis* (London: George Allen & Unwin, Ltd., 1960); R. G. Wettimuny, *Buddhism and Its Relations to Religion and Science* (Colombo: Gunasena, 1962).

21. Htoon, *The Wheel*, No. 36/37, p. 52.

22. *Ibid.*, p. 37.

23. Cited in Benz, *Buddhism or Communism . . . ?* p. 148.

24. Suriyabongs, *Buddhism in the Light of Modern Scientific Ideas*, p. 9.

25. *Ibid.*, p. 299.

26. Gordon W. Allport, *Becoming* (Yale University Press, 1955). pp. 37f.

27. King, *A Thousand Lives Away*, p. 125.

28. Ikeda, *Complete Works* . . . , Vol. I, p. 427.

29. *Ibid.*, p. 428.

30. King, *A Thousand Lives Away*, p. 126.

31. Story, *The Wheel*, No. 12/13, p. 15.

32. *Ibid.*

33. King, *A Thousand Lives Away*, p. 144.

34. Burns, *The Wheel*, No. 88/89, p. 8.

35. Suzuki, Fromm, DeMartino, *Zen Buddhism and Psychoanalysis*, p. 126.

36. *Ibid.*, pp. 123–126. Perhaps the most noted psychologist interested in Buddhism was C. J. Jung, for whom Tantric or Tibetan Buddhism held a particular fascination.

37. Burns, *The Wheel*, No. 88/89, p. 61.

38. Kasamatsu and Hirai, *Psychologia*, Vol. V, No. 4, p. 90.

39. For information on aspects of Buddhism as a world religion, see: Bechert, *Buddhismus, Staat und Gesellschaft* . . . , Vol. I, Ch. 16; Benz, *Buddhism or Communism* . . . ? Ch. II; Piyadassi Thero, "Buddhism in the Western World," Lincoln Forum Series, No. 2 (no date); Rahula, *What the Buddha Taught*, Ch. VIII; Soma Thera, "Buddhism and World Peace," *Bodhi Leaves*, No. A 13 (Kandy: Buddhist Publication Society, no date); Ven. Vinitha, "Buddhism in the United States," Lincoln Forum Series, No. 1 (no date).

40. "Looking Back and Looking Forward," Buddhist Publication Society Report, 1965, p. 7.

41. Chao Khun Sobhana Dhammasudhi conducted meditation workshops at Oberlin College during the month of January, 1969, and again in January of 1970. He was very successful in conveying to American college students the fundamental purposes and methods of Theravāda meditation.

42. *The Buddhist*, Vol. XXXVII, No. 2 (July, 1966), pp. 41–42.

43. Rahula, *What the Buddha Taught*, p. 77.

44. Soma Thera, *Bodhi Leaves*, No. A 13, p. 7.

45. These lectures have been printed under the title *The Principles of International Law in Buddhist Doctrine*. (See Chapter III, note 1, herein.)

46. Christmas Humphreys, "The Seventh Conference of the World Fellowship of Buddhists" (World Fellowship of Buddhists Secretariat, 1965), p. 11.

47. *The Buddhist,* Vol. XXXVII, No. 1 (June, 1966), pp. 1, 2.

CHAPTER IV. TWO PORTRAITS OF THAI BUDDHISM

1. Transliterated terms from the Thai generally follow Mary Hass or a common usage. Italicized words in this chapter will include both Thai and Pāli.

2. Kenneth E. Wells, *Thai Buddhism, Its Rites and Activities* (Bangkok: The Police Press, 1960), p. 268.

3. "The Mirror of the Dhamma," ed. by Narada Thera and Bhikkhu Kassapa, *The Wheel,* No. 54 (1963), p. 42.

4. The structures in a temple compound vary but a representative listing might include the *vihāra,* in which worship services are held; the *uposatha* hall or *bood,* where ordination can occur; *chedi,* or pagodalike structures which may be reliquaries or burial memorials; *kuthi,* or dwelling places for the monks; and various *saalaa,* or open assembly halls.

5. The Buddha, Dhamma, and Sangha are also called the Three Refuges. Most Buddhist services begin with the threefold chant, "I take refuge in the Buddha, the Dhamma, and the Sangha."

6. The Buddhist Sabbath is calculated according to the waning and waxing phases of the moon. In Thailand, since Sunday is the legal holiday instead of the Buddhist Sabbath, services are sometimes held on both *wan phra* and Sunday.

7. Ordinarily the Buddhist layman is expected to keep only the first five of the precepts.

8. Wells, *Thai Buddhism* . . . , p. 118.

9. Monastic studies are divided into two major sections. The first is called *naag tham* ("doctrine for the ordained") and is composed of three levels or degrees. The second division is exclusively Pāli studies and is divided into seven degrees. Outside of this structure of Sangha education stands the Buddhist university curriculum.

10. The Abhidhamma is the third division of the Pāli canon of Theravāda Buddhism and includes a variety of texts of historical, philosophical, and psychological importance. The term, however, assumes a narrower connotation in the parlance of Thai Buddhism, referring only to those texts which analyze

human existence. The most popular Abhidhamma text in Thailand is a synopsis of this philosophicopsychological literature called the Abhidhamma-ttha-Sangaha, written in Burma in the twelfth century.

11. Jasper Ingersoll, "The Priest Role in Central Village Thailand," in *Anthropological Studies in Theravāda Buddhism*, ed. by Manning Nash (Southeast Asia Studies Cultural Report Series, No. 13; Yale University, 1966), p. 63.

12. See John E. de Young, *Village Life in Modern Thailand* (University of California Press, 1958), p. 123.

13. Ingersoll, in Nash (ed.), *Anthropological Studies . . .* , pp. 57–58.

14. Herbert Phillips, *Thai Peasant Personality* (University of California Press, 1965), p. 16.

15. Howard K. Kaufman, *Bangkhuad: A Community Study in Thailand* (J. J. Augustin, Inc., Publisher, 1960), pp. 113–115.

16. Wells, *Thai Buddhism . . .* , p. 212.

17. *Ibid.*

18. *Ibid.*, p. 60.

19. See p. 113.

20. Buddhadāsa, *Khon Thyng Tham—Tham Thyng Khon*, Vol. I (Bangkok: Suwichaan, 1963), p. 27.

21. Buddhadāsa, *Rian Lad Phudthasaasanaa* (Bangkok: Organization for the Revival of Buddhism, 1963), p. 19.

22. Buddhadāsa, *Khon Thyng Tham—Tham Thyng Khon*, Vol. II (Bangkok: Suwichaan, 1963), p. 31.

23. Buddhadāsa, *Khuu Myy Manud* (Bangkok: Organization for the Revival of Buddhism, 1967), p. 18.

24. In particular, see Buddhadāsa, *Phasaa Khon—Phasaa Tham* (Thonburi: Privately published, 1967).

25. Buddhadāsa, *Khristatham—Phuthatham* (Christianity and Buddhism) (Bangkok: Group for the Propagation of the Means to a Valuable Life, 1968), pp. 35–37.

26. *Ibid.*, p. 56.

27. Buddhadāsa, *Sing Tii Raw Jang Sonjaikan N»j Pai* (Things in Which We Still Have Too Little Interest) (Chiengmai: World Fellowship of Buddhists, 1957), p. 7.

28. *Ibid.*, p. 8.

29. See Chapter I, note 11, herein.

30. Buddhadāsa, *Sing Tii Raw* . . . , p. 14.

31. In 1963 an attack on the Catholic Action Movement was published under the title *Catholic Action: A Menace to Peace and Goodwill* (Colombo: Bauddha Jatika Balavegaya, 1963). The results of this study were concluded as follows: "It would appear that surreptitiously and imperceptibly the Catholic Action Movement has captured the key positions in the Armed Forces, the Police and the Administrative Services, as well as in Agriculture, Commerce and Industry. By this means, it has succeeded in acquiring immense economic power in the land. It has gone even further. It has used its familiar technique to infiltrate into areas where Buddhism is a great force. On the one hand, it has thrown ridicule on the practices that are enjoined on Buddhism, and on the other it has put a high premium on social habits, like the drink curse, that are alien to Buddhism. . . . By actions such as these, the Catholic Action Movement has set the stage to bring Ceylon under the suzerainty of the Vatican. We are aware that it is by resorting to strategy of this sort that the Catholic Action Movement has already secured the bondage of South Vietnam, Buddhist Formosa and Buddhist Korea to the Empire of the Vatican" (p. 177).

32. *The Ceylon Daily News*, Aug. 18, 1967.

33. *Ibid.*

34. *Ibid.*

35. Soedjatmoko, "Cultural Motivations to Progress: The 'Exterior' and the 'Interior' Views," in Bellah (ed.), *Religion and Progress* . . . , p. 8.

CHAPTER V. BUDDHISM AND THE WEST

1. John B. Cobb, Jr., *The Structure of Christian Existence* (The Westminster Press, 1967), p. 148.

2. R. C. Zaehner, *Christianity and Other Religions* (Hawthorn Books, 1964), p. 8.

3. *Ibid.*, p. 40.

4. *Ibid.*, p. 38. Italics mine.

5. R. C. Zaehner, *The Comparison of Religions* (Beacon Press, 1962), p. 180.

6. Zaehner, *Christianity and Other Religions*, p. 38.

7. Wilfred Cantwell Smith, *The Meaning and End of Religion* (The Macmillan Company, 1962), pp. 154–155.

8. *Ibid.*, p. 156.

9. *Ibid.*

10. *Ibid.*

11. Wilfred Cantwell Smith, "Mankind's Religiously Divided History Approaches Self-consciousness," *The Harvard Divinity Bulletin,* 29 (October, 1964), p. 12.

12. Wilfred Cantwell Smith, *The Meaning and End of Religion,* p. 141.

13. *Ibid.*, p. 135.

14. *Ibid.*, p. 128.

15. Joachim Wach, *The Comparative Study of Religions* (Columbia University Press, 1961), pp. 30 f.

16. Wilfred Cantwell Smith, *The Meaning and End of Religion,* pp. 170–185.

17. *Ibid.*, p. 183. Italics mine.

18. *Ibid.*, p. 129.

19. Wilfred Cantwell Smith, *The Harvard Divinity Bulletin,* 29 (October, 1964), p. 8.

20. Wilfred Cantwell Smith, *The Faith of Other Men* (New American Library, 1963), p. 76.

21. Ninian Smart, *A Dialogue of Religions* (London: SCM Press, Ltd., 1960), p. 9.

22. Wilfred Cantwell Smith, *Questions of Religious Truth* (Charles Scribner's Sons, 1967), p. 69.

23. *Ibid.*, p. 68. Italics mine.

24. *Ibid.*, p. 70.

25. Wilfred Cantwell Smith, "Religious Atheism? Early Buddhist and Recent American," reprint from *MILLA wa-MILLA,* Vol. VI (1966), p. 12.

26. *Ibid.*, p. 13.

27. Zaehner, *Christianity and Other Religions,* p. 31. Italics mine.

28. Wilfred Cantwell Smith, *MILLA wa-MILLA,* Vol. VI (1966), p. 8.

29. *Ibid.*, p. 10.

30. Father Merton's books on Asian religions include *The Way of Chuang-tzu, Mystics and Zen Masters* and *Zen and the Birds of Appetite.*

31. Thomas Merton, *Zen and the Birds of Appetite* (New Directions, 1968), p. 47.

32. *Ibid.*, p. 44.

33. *Ibid.*, p. 13.

34. *Ibid.*, p. 8.

35. Dom Aelred Graham, *Zen Catholicism* (Harcourt, Brace and World, Inc., 1963), p. 44.

36. *Ibid.*, p. 157.

37. See Thomas J. J. Altizer, *Oriental Mysticism and Biblical Eschatology* (The Westminster Press, 1961), Chs. 4 to 5.

38. The four works are *Behold the Spirit* (1947), *The Supreme Identity* (1950), *Myth and Ritual in Christianity* (1953), and *Beyond Theology: The Art of Godmanship* (1964).

39. Alan Watts, *This Is It* (Collier Books, 1967), p. 48.

40. Alan Watts, *Beyond Theology: The Art of Godmanship* (Pantheon Books, 1964), p. 222.

41. Watts, *This Is It*, pp. 56–57.

42. *Ibid.*, p. 50.

43. See Alan Watts, *The Wisdom of Insecurity* (Vintage Books, Random House, Inc., 1968).

44. Winston L. King, *Buddhism and Christianity: Some Bridges of Understanding* (The Westminster Press, 1962), pp. 195 f. See also the entirety of Ch. VI therein.